SOUND INNOVATIONS

SOUND DEVELOPMENT
Warm-up Exercises for Tone and Technique
INTERMEDIATE STRING ORCHESTRA

Bob **PHILLIPS** | Kirk **MOSS**

Sound Innovations: Sound Development emphasizes playing with a characteristic beautiful sound. What goes into producing this sound is broken into four levels, consistent with the revolutionary *Sound Innovations* structure: **(1) Sound Tone**; **(2) Sound Bowings**; **(3) Sound Shifting**; and **(4) Sound Scales, Arpeggios, Chorales, and Rhythms**. The levels can be used in the order that is best for your development, whether that means as individual warm-ups or as structured units. Video demonstrations of key skills are indicated by and can be viewed at alfred.com/SoundDevelopmentVideo.

Level 1: Sound Tone
More than just scales and arpeggios, this method builds sequences upon some of the most important variables of sound: bowing lanes, bow weight, and bow speed. Level 1 contains a sequential development of the skills that affect tone production, with easy-to-teach-and-play warm-up exercises. Use these practice opportunities to develop an excellent tone.

Level 2: Sound Bowings
A string player's right-hand technique is often called his or her voice. This level will help develop a sound-driven technique, focusing on right-hand skills. Complete pedagogical sequences of the right-hand skills are presented as self-contained units with careful attention to detail. Refine hooked bowings, articulate martelé and spiccato, and learn collé with a comprehensive presentation of bowing (attack strokes). Level 2 can be studied sequentially or as repertoire requires.

Level 3: Sound Shifting
Shifting techniques are introduced through harmonics, and positions are thoroughly presented using finger patterns. This level contains an extremely thorough unison presentation of 3rd through 5th position for all instruments, making it easy to teach and learn shifting in a heterogeneous class. It also provides a solid introduction to 2nd and 4th positions. Clearly notated transport/guide fingers and finger-pattern logic allow a structured understanding of shifting. The fingering chart is strategically placed within this section for a quick visual reference.

Level 4: Scales, Arpeggios, Chorales, and Rhythms
Scales, arpeggios, and broken thirds are presented in all keys up through three sharps and three flats. The innovative format is flexible, allowing each section or player to play one or two octaves while the ensemble either plays the same or different octaves. Each scale has a traditional fingering above the notes and an alternate fingering below the notes. Harmonized string orchestra and drone accompaniment lines are provided, as well as chorales and rhythm exercises in a variety of meters.

© 2012 Alfred Music Publishing Co., Inc.
Sound Innovations™ is a trademark of Alfred Music Publishing Co., Inc.
All Rights Reserved including Public Performance

ISBN-10: 0-7390-6801-6
ISBN-13: 978-0-7390-6801-4

Instrument photos courtesy of Yamaha Corporation of America Band & Orchestral Division

Level 1: Sound Tone
Bowing Lanes

A **BOWING LANE** is the area between the fingerboard and bridge where the bow is placed:

 View video at
alfred.com/SoundDevelopmentVideo

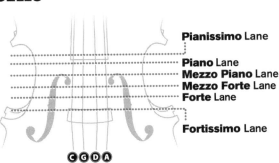

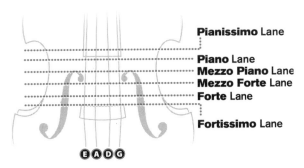

1 **PLAYING IN THE MEZZO FORTE (*mf*) LANE**—*Place your bow in the* mezzo forte (*mf*) *lane slightly toward the bridge.*

SOUND ADVICE

Remind students to keep the bow parallel to the bridge.

2 **PLAYING IN THE FORTE (f) LANE**—*Place your bow in the* forte *(f) lane near the bridge.*

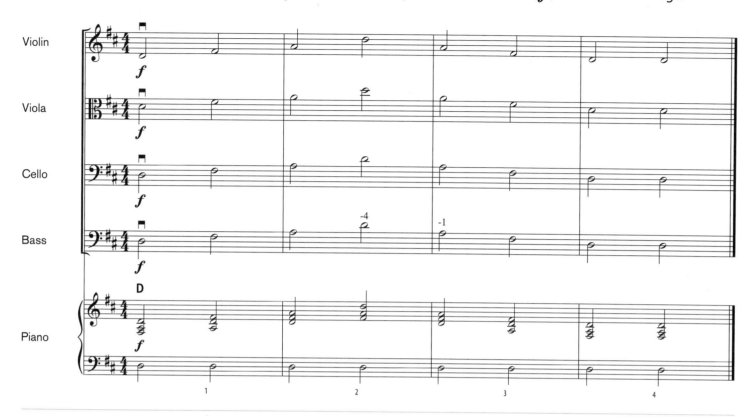

SOUND ADVICE

Remind students to start the bow near the frog.

TILTING THE STICK

Tilt the stick of the bow by rolling it slightly toward the scroll. Only the edge of the hair will now contact the string.

View video at
alfred.com/SoundDevelopmentVideo

VIOLIN/VIOLA   **CELLO/BASS**

3 **PLAYING IN THE MEZZO PIANO (*mp*) LANE**—*Place your bow in the* mezzo piano (*mp*) *lane slightly toward the fingerboard and tilt your bow toward the scroll.*

SOUND ADVICE

Remind students to tilt the the bow toward the scroll.

4 **PLAYING IN THE PIANO (*p*) LANE**—*Place your bow in the* piano (*p*) *lane near the fingerboard and tilt the bow stick toward the scroll. Play in the middle section of the bow.*

SOUND ADVICE

Remind students to tilt the the bow toward the scroll.

5   **PLAYING IN THE FORTISSIMO ($\boldsymbol{ff}$) LANE**—*Place your bow in the fortissimo ($\boldsymbol{ff}$) lane very near the bridge and use flat bow hair. Be sure to move the bow slowly and save bow in the last two measures.*

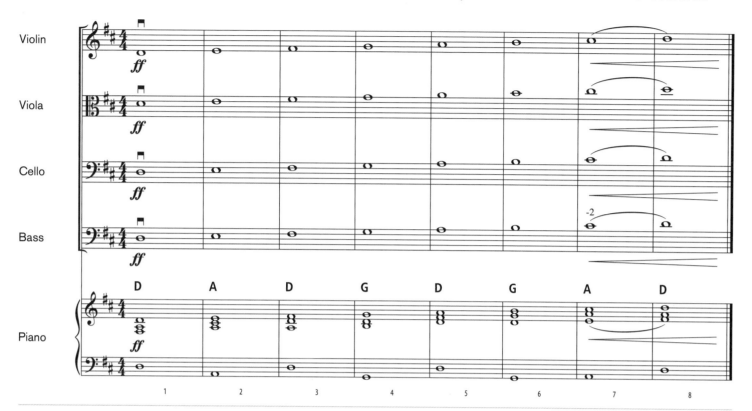

SOUND ADVICE

Remind students to use flat bow hair.

6   **PLAYING IN THE PIANISSIMO ($\boldsymbol{pp}$) LANE**—*Place your bow in the pianissimo ($\boldsymbol{pp}$) lane very near the fingerboard and tilt your bow stick toward the scroll. Challenge: Perform* Playing in the Fortissimo Lane *and* Playing in the Pianissimo Lane *as one piece.*

SOUND ADVICE

Remind students to tilt the bow toward the scroll.

Level 1: Sound Tone
Bowing Lanes

PARALLEL BOWING—Set your bow on the D string at the midpoint of the bow. Push your right hand away from your head and then toward your head in a rowing motion. Pushing your right hand away from you creates an X where the bow hair and the string intersect. Pulling the bow towards you creates an X also. Push or pull the right hand until the bow hair makes a perfect T with the string so it is perpendicular to the string and parallel to the bridge. Keeping the bow perpendicular to the string and parallel to the bridge helps create a beautiful tone.

 View video at
alfred.com/SoundDevelopmentVideo

7   **ROW YOUR BOW**—*Row your bow back and forth during each measure of rest and then stop when it is perpendicular to the string and parallel to the bridge.*

SOUND ADVICE

Remind students to start with the bow parallel to the bridge.

8 **CHANGING BOWING LANES**—*Gradually move the bow from the* pianissimo *(**pp**) to the* fortissimo *(**ff**) bowing lane and back. Remember to keep your bow parallel to the bridge. Challenge: Go back and play the exercise starting up bow.*

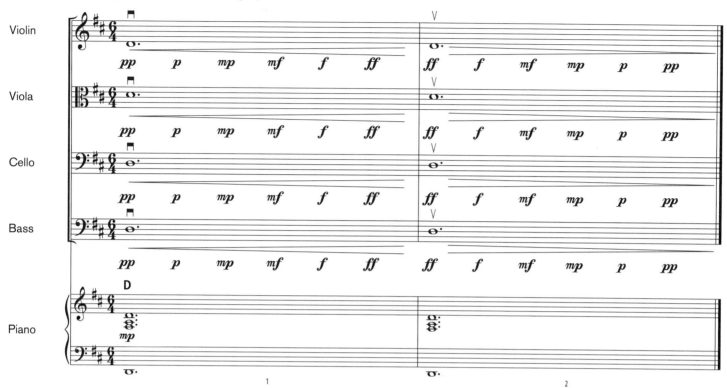

SOUND ADVICE

Remind students to move the bow slowly.

9 **CHANGING BOWING LANES IN ONE BOW**—*Move from the* pianissimo *(**pp**) to the* fortissimo *(**ff**) bowing lane and back all in one bow. Remember to keep your bow parallel to the bridge. Challenge: Go back and play the exercise starting up bow.*

SOUND ADVICE

Remind students to start with the bow parallel to the bridge.

10   THEME FROM SYMPHONY NO. 104, MVT. 4—*Practice changing from the mezzo forte (mf) to the forte (f) bowing lane.*

Joseph Haydn

SOUND ADVICE

Remind students to change bowing lanes when changing dynamics.

11 **COSSACK LULLABY**—*Practice changing from the piano (**p**) to the pianissimo (**pp**) bowing lane. Compare and contrast the musical elements of Cossack Lullaby from the Romantic period of music and Theme from Symphony No. 104 from the Classical period of music.*

Russian Folk Song

SOUND ADVICE

Remind students to change bowing lanes when changing dynamics.

Level 1: Sound Tone
Bow Weight

BOW WEIGHT is the amount of pressure applied to the string using the right arm and hand. Weight causes the bow to sink into the string.

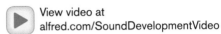 View video at alfred.com/SoundDevelopmentVideo

VIOLIN/VIOLA   **CELLO**

BASS

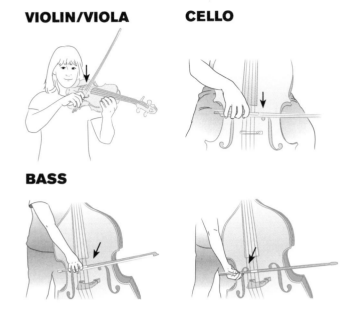

12   **MEDIUM-HEAVY BOW WEIGHT**—*Place your bow in the* mezzo forte *(**mf**) lane and play with a medium-heavy amount of arm weight in the bow. Play with flat bow hair. Challenge: Go back and play the exercise in a two-part round (group A and B) as your teacher directs.*

SOUND ADVICE

Remind students to keep the right-hand fingers relaxed while adding or removing arm weight.

13 **HEAVY BOW WEIGHT**—*Place your bow in the* forte (*f*) *lane and play with a heavy amount of arm weight in the bow. Play with flat bow hair.*

SOUND ADVICE

Remind students to keep the right-hand fingers relaxed while adding or removing arm weight.

14 **VERY-HEAVY BOW WEIGHT**—*Place your bow in the* fortissimo (*ff*) *lane and play with a very heavy amount of arm weight in the bow. Play with flat bow hair. Be sure to move the bow slowly (save bow) in the last two bars.*

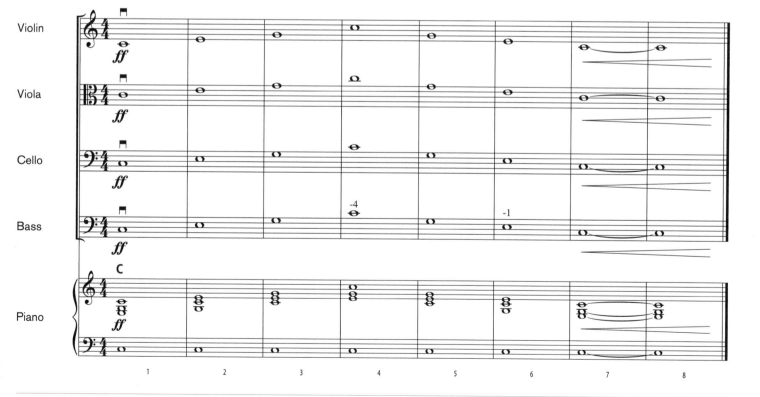

SOUND ADVICE

Remind students to keep the right-hand fingers relaxed while adding or removing arm weight.

15 **MEDIUM-LIGHT BOW WEIGHT**—*Place your bow in the* mezzo piano *(mp) lane and play with a medium-light amount of hand weight in the bow. Play in the middle of the bow. Tilt the bow.*

SOUND ADVICE

Remind students to keep the right-hand fingers relaxed while adding or removing arm weight.

16 **LIGHT BOW WEIGHT**—*Place your bow in the* piano *(p) lane and play with a light amount of hand weight in the bow. Play in the upper half of the bow. Tilt the bow.*

SOUND ADVICE

Remind students to keep the right-hand fingers relaxed while adding or removing arm weight.

17   **VERY-LIGHT BOW WEIGHT**—*Place your bow in the* pianissimo *(pp) lane and play with a very light amount of hand weight in the bow. Play near the tip of the bow. Tilt the bow.*

SOUND ADVICE

Remind students to keep the right-hand fingers relaxed while adding or removing arm weight.

Level 1: Sound Tone
Bow Weight

18 **DYNAMIC CONTRAST**—*Practice using a heavy bow weight and a light bow weight. Release any tension in your bow-hand fingers during the rests.*

SOUND ADVICE

Remind students to keep the right-hand fingers relaxed while adding or removing arm weight.

RELEASING BOW WEIGHT EXERCISE

1. Set the middle of the bow on the D string.
2. Transfer your arm weight through your wrist, hand and evenly amongst your fingers.
3. Allow the bow stick to sink toward the string.
4. Release the weight and feel the natural spring of the bow stick.

 View video at alfred.com/SoundDevelopmentVideo

VIOLIN/VIOLA

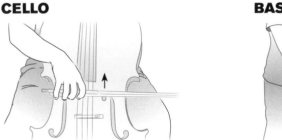

CELLO

BASS

Leopold Mozart (the father of Wolfgang Amadeus Mozart) taught a variation of this exercise in the 18th century. Use bow strokes that change from loud in the first part of the stroke to soft in the second part. See how deeply you can sink the bow into the string without breaking the tone. Feel the give of the wood of the bow, the hair and the string. Avoid an accent, scratch, or bite at the start of the tone.

19 **PULSING TONE**—*Practice changing from a medium-heavy to a light bow weight while staying in the mezzo forte (mf) bowing lane.*

SOUND ADVICE

Remind students to keep the right-hand fingers relaxed while adding or removing arm weight.

20 **DEEP TONE, PULSE TONE**—*Practice pulsing the bow.*

SOUND ADVICE

Remind students to keep the right-hand fingers relaxed while adding or removing arm weight.

21 **FRENCH FOLK SONG**—*Practice playing this portion of* French Folk Song *with three pulses per measure.*
Challenge: Play the rest of the song by ear.

Traditional

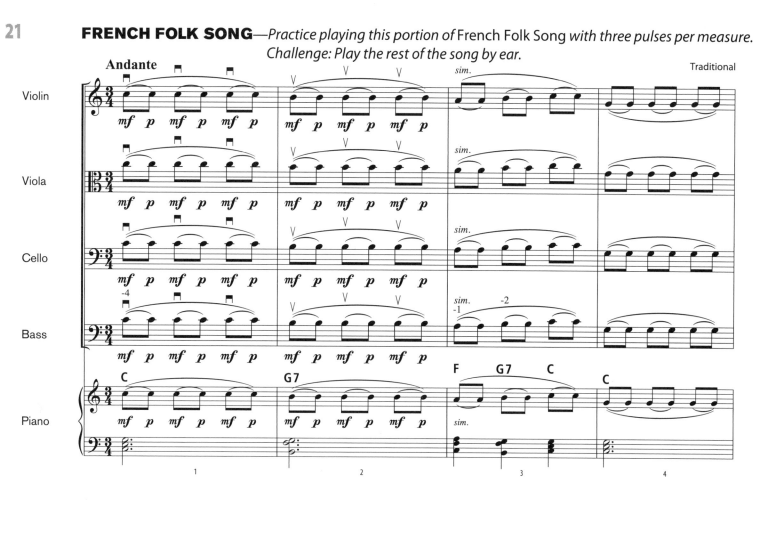

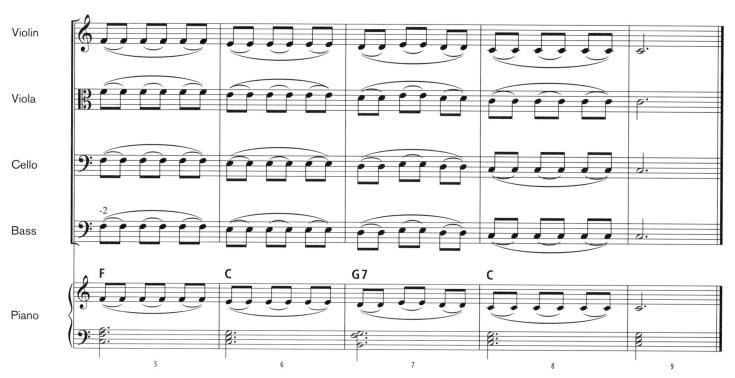

SOUND ADVICE

Remind students to keep the right-hand fingers relaxed while adding or removing arm weight.

Level 1: Sound Tone
Bow Speed

BOW SPEED is how fast or slow the bow moves across the string. Expressive playing employs a range of bow speeds from very fast to very slow.

 View video at
alfred.com/SoundDevelopmentVideo

MAELZEL'S METRONOME, abbreviated M.M., uses a number which indicates the number of beats per minute on the metronome. It is often shown with a note value in place of M.M. ($\quarternote = 80$). Use a metronome to keep a steady tempo and play each of the exercises below at ($\quarternote = 80$).

22 **MEDIUM-FAST BOW SPEED**—*Place your bow in the* mezzo piano *(mp) lane with a medium-light amount of hand weight and move the bow at a medium-fast bow speed.*

SOUND ADVICE

Remind students to keep the bow parallel to the bridge while adjusting the tone variables.

23 **MEDIUM-SLOW BOW SPEED**—*Place your bow in the* mezzo forte *(**mf**) lane with a medium-heavy amount of arm weight and move the bow at a medium-slow bow speed.*

SOUND ADVICE

Remind students to keep the bow parallel to the bridge while adjusting the tone variables.

24 **SLOW BOW SPEED**—*Place your bow in the* forte *(**f**) lane with a heavy amount of arm weight and move the bow at a slow bow speed.*

SOUND ADVICE

Remind students to keep the bow parallel to the bridge while adjusting the tone variables.

25 **VERY-SLOW BOW SPEED**—*Place your bow in the* fortissimo (*ff*) *lane with a very-heavy amount of arm weight and move the bow at a very-slow bow speed. Challenge: Play this piece slurring four measures in one bow.*

SOUND ADVICE

Remind students to keep the bow parallel to the bridge while adjusting the tone variables.

26 **FAST BOW SPEED**—*Place your bow in the* piano (*p*) *lane, play with a light amount of hand weight and move the bow at a fast bow speed. Play in the middle of the bow.*

SOUND ADVICE

Remind students to keep the bow parallel to the bridge while adjusting the tone variables.

27   **VERY-FAST BOW SPEED**—*Place your bow in the* pianissimo *(pp) lane, play with a very-light amount of hand weight and move the bow at a very-fast bow speed. Play near the tip of the bow.*

SOUND ADVICE

Remind students to keep the bow parallel to the bridge while adjusting the tone variables.

Level 1: Sound Tone
Bow Speed

28   **CHANGING FROM SLOW TO FAST BOW SPEED**—*Move the bow slowly on the first three beats of each measure with a medium bow weight. Each 4th beat will be played with a fast bow speed. The up bow will travel in one beat as far as the down bow travels in three beats.*

SOUND ADVICE

Remind students to use a whole bow.

29 **CHANGING FROM FAST TO SLOW BOW SPEED**—*Move the bow quickly on beat 1 of each measure with a light bow weight. Each down bow will last one beat while the up bow will travel the same distance in three beats.*

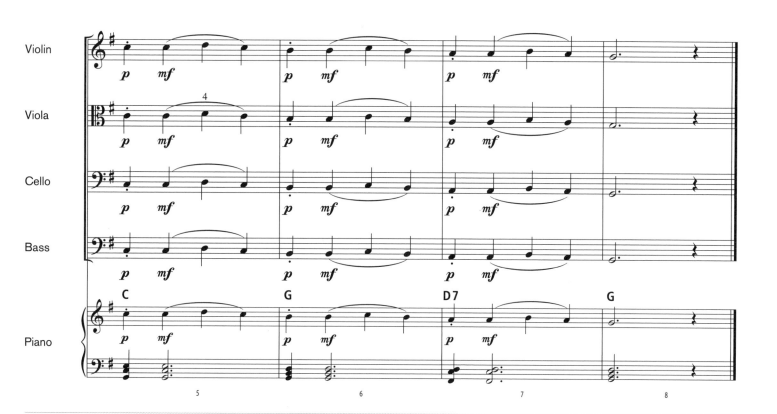

SOUND ADVICE

Remind students to use a whole bow.

30 **SAVE AND SPEND THE BOW**—*Play the first three beats using only 1/3 of the bow and beat 4 using the remaining 2/3.*

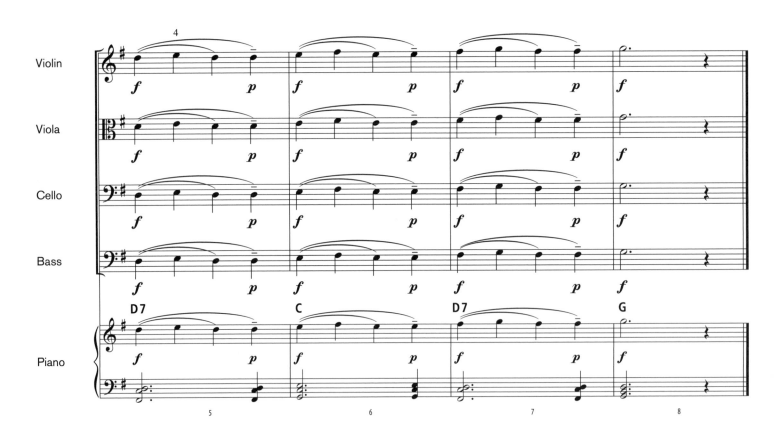

SOUND ADVICE

Remind students to use a whole bow.

USING DIFFERENT PARTS OF THE BOW

The whole bow can be divided into three parts:
the *lower* third, the *middle* third and the *upper* third.

VIOLIN/VIOLA

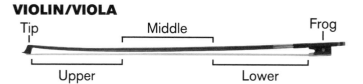

CELLO

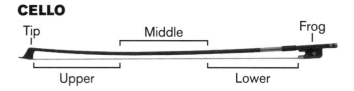

BASS

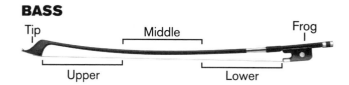

31 **SAKURA**—*Practice playing at the tip, upper third, middle third, lower third and frog of the bow. On the measures marked crawl, use a faster bow speed to move to a different part of the bow.*

SOUND ADVICE

Remind students to divide the bow into three equal sections.

Level 1: Sound Tone
Bow Division

USING DIFFERENT PARTS OF THE BOW

The whole bow can be divided into three parts:
the *lower* third, the *middle* third and the *upper* third.

 View video at
alfred.com/SoundDevelopmentVideo

VIOLIN/VIOLA

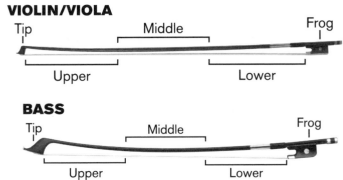

CELLO

BASS

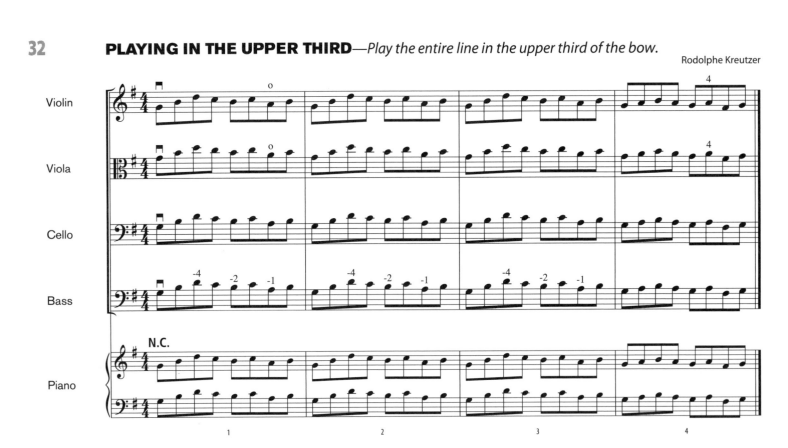

32 **PLAYING IN THE UPPER THIRD**—*Play the entire line in the upper third of the bow.*

Rodolphe Kreutzer

Violin

Viola

Cello

Bass

Piano

SOUND ADVICE

Remind students to divide the bow into three equal sections.

33 **PLAYING IN THE MIDDLE THIRD**—*Play the entire line in the middle third of the bow.*

SOUND ADVICE

Remind students to divide the bow into three equal sections.

34 **PLAYING IN THE LOWER THIRD**—*Play the entire line in the lower third of the bow.*

SOUND ADVICE

Remind students to divide the bow into three equal sections.

35 **MOVING FROM FROG TO TIP**—*Start in the lower third of the bow and gradually crawl to the upper third of the bow.*

SOUND ADVICE

Remind students to divde the bow into three equal parts.

36 **MOVING FROM TIP TO FROG**—*Start in the upper third of the bow and gradually crawl to the lower third of the bow.*

SOUND ADVICE

Remind students to divide the bow into three equal sections.

37 **PLAYING WITH A WHOLE BOW**—*Use a whole bow on each note. Be sure to move the bow slowly (save bow) in the last measure. Challenge: Go back and play the entire page as one piece.*

SOUND ADVICE

Remind students to divide the bow into three equal sections.

Level 1: Sound Tone
Tone Repertoire

38   **THE GREAT GATE OF KIEV**—*Start in the* forte (𝑓) *lane with a heavy bow weight moving at a slow speed. Adjust the tone variables as needed throughout the piece. Then describe the adjustments you made. Listen to a recording of a professional performance of this piece and analyze how the players control the tone variables when they play.*

Modest Mussorgsky

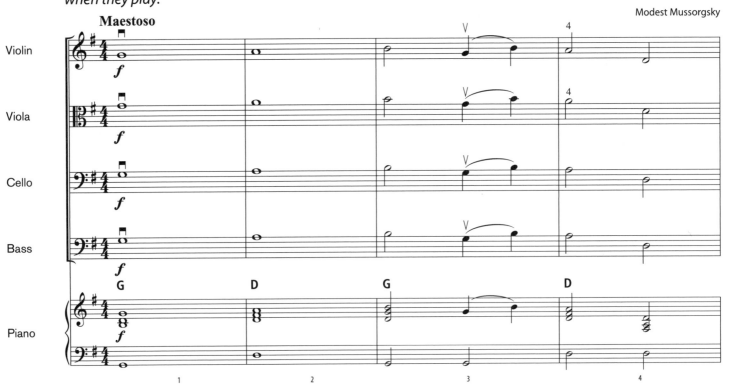

SOUND ADVICE
Remind students to move the bow slowly (save the bow) on the whole notes.

THEME FROM SYMPHONY NO. 1—*Start in the* mezzo forte (*mf*) *lane with a medium-heavy bow weight moving at medium-slow speed. Adjust the tone variables as needed throughout the piece. Then describe the adjustments you made. Listen to a professional recording of this piece and compare your performance to it.*

SOUND ADVICE

Remind students to save the bow on the dotted half note.

40 **ARIRANG**—*Start in the* pianissimo *(**pp**) lane with a very-light bow weight moving at a very-fast speed. Adjust the tone variables as needed throughout the piece. How does adjusting tone variables compare to the use of color in the visual arts?*

Korean Folk Song

SOUND ADVICE

Remind students to adjust the right-arm level when crossing strings.

41 **CRIPPLE CREEK**—*Start in the* mezzo forte *lane with a medium-weight bow moving at a medium-slow speed. Adjust the tone variables as needed throughout the piece. Then describe the adjustments you made.*

American Fiddle Tune

Challenge 1: Listen to each piece of music above and decide the style and which historical period it's from.
Challenge 2: Use the tone variables you have learned in Level 1 to play songs from various cultures and time periods
that you learned in Sound Innovations *books 1 and 2.*

SOUND ADVICE

Remind students to adjust the level of the right arm when crossing strings.

Level 2: Sound Bowings
Detaché

DETACHÉ–Separate bow strokes played smoothly with an evenness of tone. *Sound Advice:* Keep the bow parallel to the bridge.

BOW WRITING EXERCISE

1. Hold the bow in a vertical position.
2. While sitting, lean forward and rest your right forearm on your leg.
3. Allow your right wrist to extend past your knee.
4. Pretend the adjusting screw of the bow is a pencil.
5. Use the flexible joints in the wrist, fingers, and thumb to write your signature in the air.
6. Avoid tilting the stick as you write.

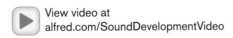 View video at
alfred.com/SoundDevelopmentVideo

DETACHÉ BOWING ABOVE AND BELOW THE MIDDLE OF THE BOW

Move your right arm smoothly by using a flexible elbow.

VIOLIN/VIOLA   **CELLO**   **BASS**

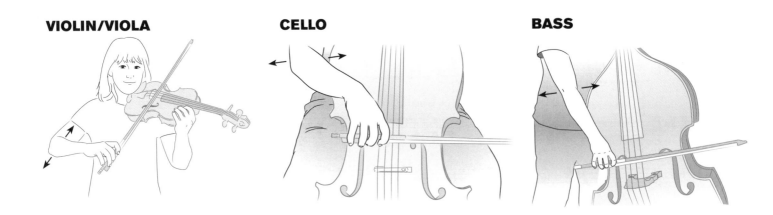

42 **PAVANNE**—*Start in the piano (p) lane with a light bow weight and a medium-fast bow speed. Move your right arm smoothly to create a beautiful detaché stroke.*

French Renaissance Dance

SOUND ADVICE

Remind students to use a flexible right-hand wrist when changing bow directions.

DETACHÉ BOWING USING HAND AND WRIST MOVEMENT
Move your bow smoothly by using your wrist and fingers.

HAND AND WRIST MOVEMENT EXERCISE
1. Hold your right hand loosely in front of you.
2. Let your right-hand fingers dangle.
3. Use your right hand as if it is a paint brush and paint your music stand.
4. Let your right-hand fingers move back and forth like the bristles on the brush.

VIOLIN/VIOLA

CELLO

BASS

43 **CREDO FROM MASS NO. 2, EXCERPT 1**—*Start in the* mezzo forte (*mf*) *lane with a medium-heavy bow weight and a fast bow speed. Use a flexible wrist and fingers to play a detaché stroke on each eighth note.*

Franz Schubert

SOUND ADVICE

Remind students to look through the piece for any written accidentals before playing.

Level 2: Sound Bowings
Tremolo

TREMOLO–Separate bow strokes played as quickly as possible.
Sound Advice: Play near the tip for softer dynamic levels.

44 **PLAYING TREMOLO**—*Starting in the upper part of the bow accelerate the bow speed through each measure until you are playing* tremolo *in measure 4.*

SOUND ADVICE

Remind students to keep the right-hand wrist relaxed as they play tremolo.

45   **THEME OF THE BAD GUYS**—*Start in the* piano (*p*) *lane with a light bow weight and move the bow as quickly as possible for the* tremolo. *Change the bowing lanes and crawl the bow as needed. Describe what you changed.*

SOUND ADVICE

Remind students to play tremolo in the upper half of the bow.

STACCATO—Bow strokes that stop and release the sound after each note creating a separation or space between notes. *Sound Advice:* Keep the bow weight even through the note.

View video at
alfred.com/SoundDevelopmentVideo

46 **LEARNING TO PLAY STACCATO**—*Practice going from* detaché *to staccato* bowing in the middle third of the bow.

SOUND ADVICE

Remind students to release the staccato notes without crunching the sound.

47 **CREDO FROM MASS NO. 2, EXCERPT 2**—*Practice playing* staccato *in the lower third of the bow.*

Franz Schubert

SOUND ADVICE

Remind students to stay in the lower third of the bow.

Level 2: Sound Bowings
Staccato Hooks

STACCATO HOOKS—Two or more stopped strokes that are played in the same bow direction and are usually notated with slurs. *Sound Advice:* Each note should have a bell tone that rings and then decays.

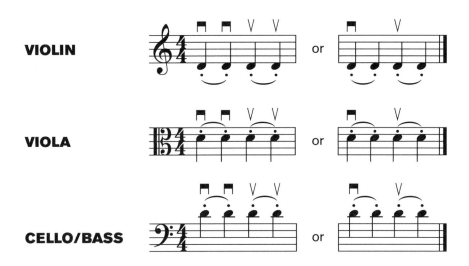

48   **LEARNING TO PLAY STACCATO HOOKS**—*Starting in the lower third of the bow, be careful to stop the bow and release the sound after each staccato note.*

SOUND ADVICE

Remind students to feel the pulse of the right-hand thumb when playing hooked staccatos.

49 **PLAYING STACCATO HOOKS**—*Starting in the lower third of the bow, practice playing* staccato *hooks.*

SOUND ADVICE

Remind students to feel the pulse of the right-hand thumb when playing hooked staccatos.

50 **PACK SHE BACK TO SHE MA**—*Starting in the lower third of the bow, practice playing* staccato *hooks.*
Challenge: Circle the staccato *hooked notes.*

Barbados Folk Song

SOUND ADVICE

Remind students to stop the bow on the hooked down bows.

51 **CABBAGE AND BEETS**—*Starting in the lower third of the bow, be careful to stop the bow and release the sound after each staccato note.*

German Folk Song

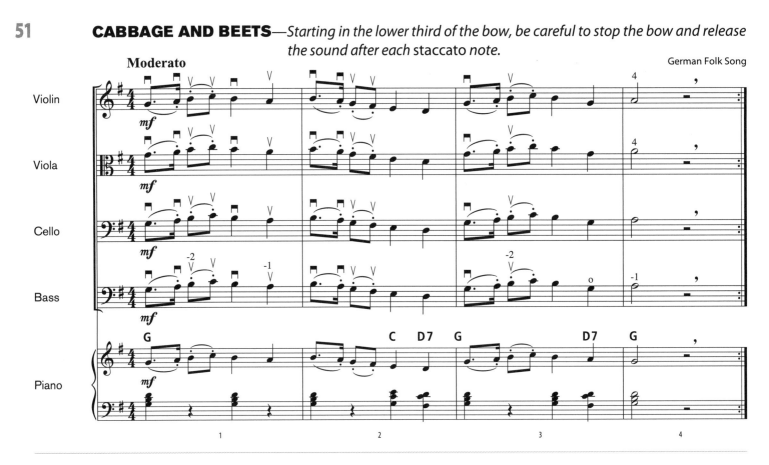

SOUND ADVICE

Remind students to stop the bow and release the sound between each series of staccato hooked bows.

52 **NON PIÙ ANDRAI**—*Starting in the middle third of the bow, practice playing* staccato *hooked bowings.*
Be careful to play the rhythms accurately.

Wolfgang Amadeus Mozart

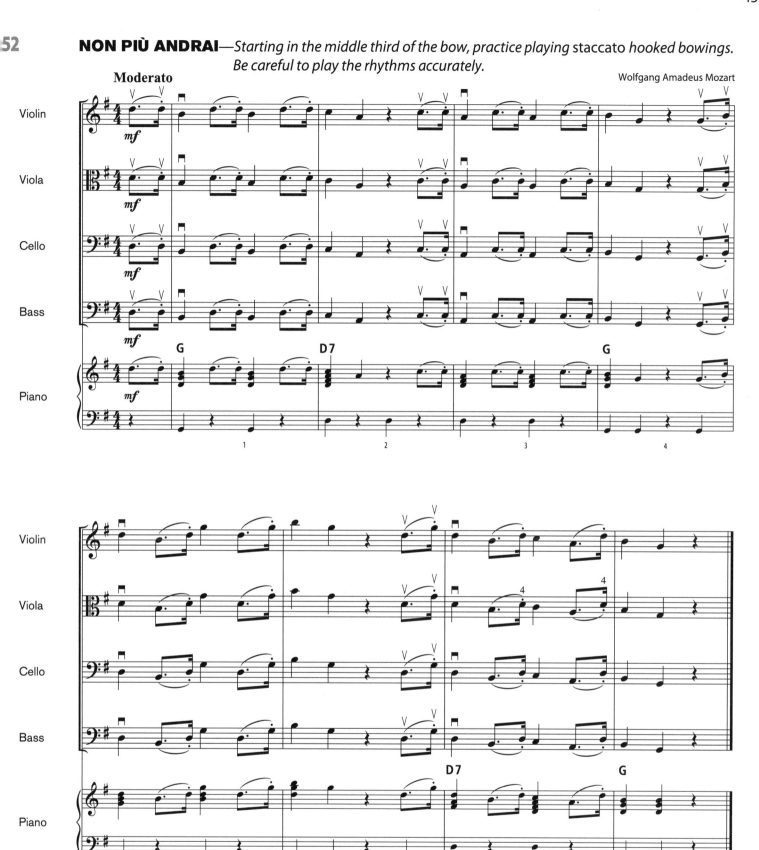

SOUND ADVICE

Remind students to stop the bow and release the sound between each series of staccato hooked bows.

Level 2: Sound Bowings
Legato Hooks

TENUTO—To hold a note for its full value, indicated by a line over or under the note.

LEGATO HOOKS—Two or more legato strokes played in the same bow direction called **PORTATO (LOURÉ)**. *Sound Advice:* Each note should have a pulsed tone.

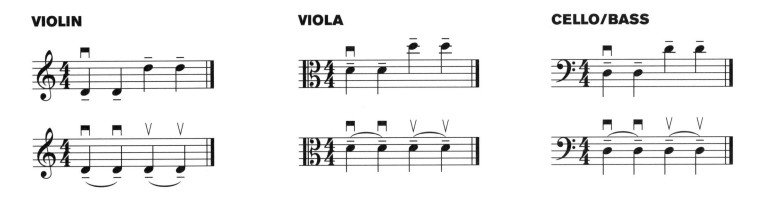

53 **LEARNING TO PLAY LEGATO HOOKS**—*Be careful to play smoothly.*

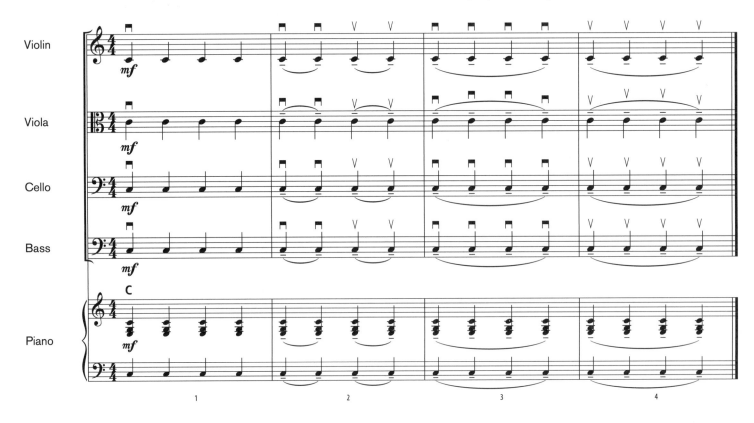

SOUND ADVICE

Remind students to play the legato hooked bowings with a smooth pulsation.

ALLEGRO CON BRIO FROM SYMPHONY NO. 1—*Practice playing* legato *hooked quarter notes.*

54

Ludwig van Beethoven

SOUND ADVICE

Remind students to play the legato hooked bowings with a smooth pulsation.

55 **PLAYING LEGATO HOOKED EIGHTH NOTES**—*Practice playing* legato *hooked eighth notes.*

SOUND ADVICE

Remind students to play the legato hooked bowings with a smooth pulsation.

56 **THEME FROM KEYBOARD CONCERTO**—*Play using* legato *hooked bowings.*

Johann Sebastian Bach

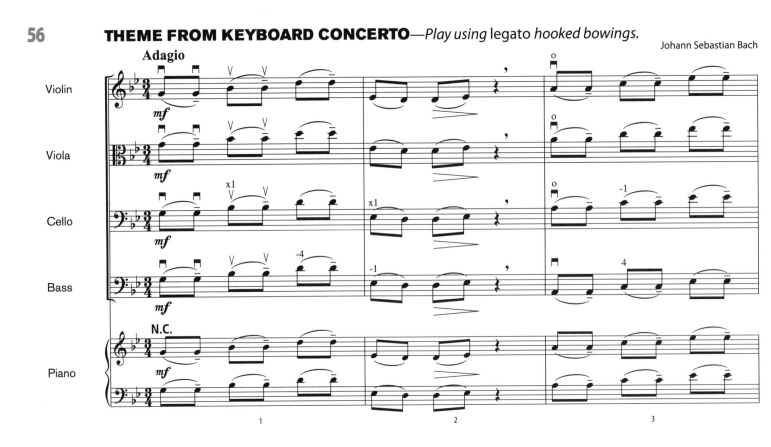

SOUND ADVICE

Remind students to play the legato hooked bowings with a smooth pulsation.

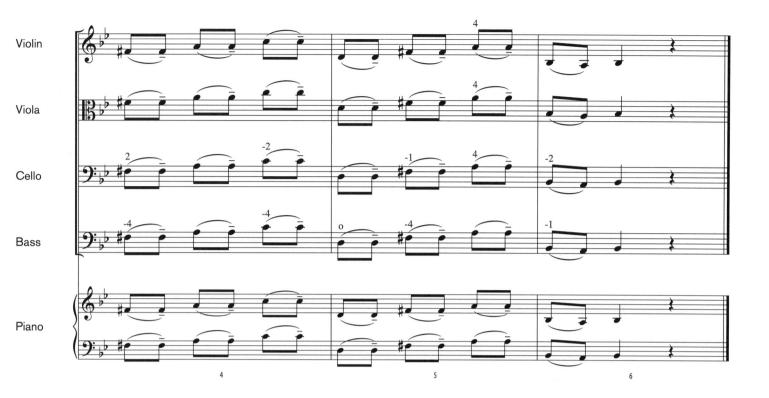

Level 2: Sound Bowings
Martelé

MARTELÉ

MARTELÉ–Separate bow strokes that start with weight in the bow to create a crisp attack. The weight is partially released as the note starts. The bow stops and releases the sound at the end of the note. *Sound Advice:* Use heavy-light bow weight and fast-slow bow speed.

 View video at alfred.com/SoundDevelopmentVideo

STRING WIGGLE EXERCISE–Pinch the bow into the string so the hair grips the string and wiggles it, silently pulling the string from side to side (↔). Feel the spring in the bow stick.

THE CLICK EXERCISE–Play *martelé* with a fast-slow bow speed. Release the pressure (weight) the instant the bow moves and listen for the "click" at the beginning.

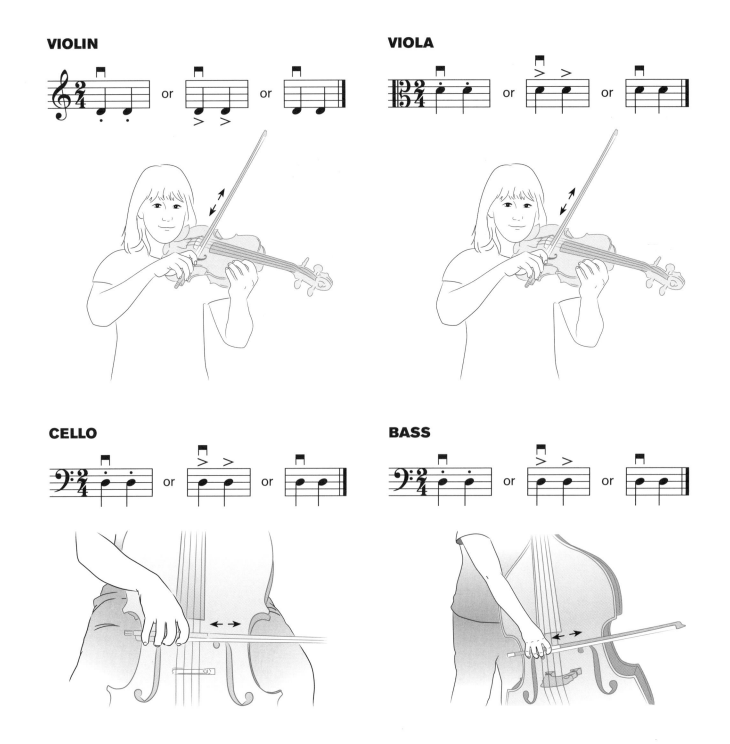

57 **LEARNING TO PLAY MARTELÉ**—*During each rest, wiggle the string back and forth using flexible fingers on the bow. Use the* martelé *stroke on each quarter note.*

SOUND ADVICE

Remind students to listen for the click at the beginning of each note.

58 **PLAYING MARTELÉ ON TWO QUARTER NOTES**—*During each rest, wiggle the string back and forth using flexible fingers on the bow. Use the* martelé *stroke on each quarter note.*

SOUND ADVICE

Have students play the exercise pizzicato, then arco and compare the ring.

Level 2: Sound Bowings
Martelé

59   **PLAYING MARTELÉ ON THE C SCALE**—*Practice using the* martelé *bow stroke on each note of the C scale in the middle of the bow. Challenge: Play this exercise using different dynamic levels and sections of the bow.*

SOUND ADVICE

Remind students to pinch into the string before moving the bow.

60 **BRITISH GRENADIERS**—*Start in the* forte (*f*) *lane with heavy bow weight and use the* martelé *bow stroke in the middle of the bow.*

English Folk Song

SOUND ADVICE

Remind students to pinch into the string before moving the bow.

61 **LEARNING TO PLAY WITH A FAST MARTELÉ**—*Start in the piano (p) lane using the upper third of the bow with a light bow weight moving the bow very fast on each eighth note.*

SOUND ADVICE

Remind students to release the bow weight as soon as they move the bow.

62 **PLAYING WITH A FAST MARTELÉ ON EIGHTH NOTES**—*Start in the mezzo piano (mp) lane using the upper third of the bow with a medium-light bow weight and move the bow very fast on each eighth note.*

SOUND ADVICE

Remind students to release the bow weight as soon as they move the bow.

63   **GLORIA**—*Play* martelé *by starting in the middle of the bow in the* mezzo piano *(* **mp** *) lane with a medium-lig* *bow weight and move the bow very fast on each eighth note. Listen to a professional recording of this piece and develop a musical checklist to compare and evaluate your performance.*

Antonio Vivaldi

SOUND ADVICE

Remind students to play the legato hooked bowings with a smooth pulsation.

Level 2: Sound Bowings
Collé

COLLÉ—A sharply pinched-attack bow stroke that is lifted off the string in a scoop motion, sometimes called a bowed pizzicato. *Sound Advice:* Use finger action to lift and set the bow.

 View video at alfred.com/SoundDevelopmentVideo

BOW PULL-UP EXERCISE
1. Hold the bow in a vertical position.
2. While sitting, lean forward and rest your right forearm on your leg.
3. Allow your wrist to extend past your knee.
4. Use finger action to pull the bow half an inch upward. Notice how the knuckles bend and fingers curve.
5. Return the bow downward to its starting point. Notice how the fingers straighten.
6. Repeat this motion several times.

 View video at alfred.com/SoundDevelopmentVideo

FROG AND TIP COLLÉ

VIOLIN

VIOLA

CELLO

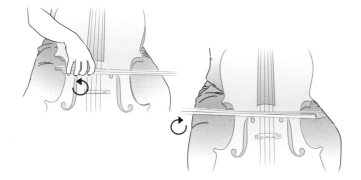

BASS

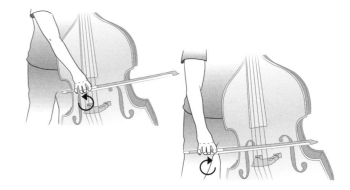

64 **COLLÉ EXERCISE**—*During the first rest, set/pinch the bow into the string in the lower third of the bow. Wiggle the string with the bow and then flick the bow off the string.*

SOUND ADVICE

Remind students to release the bow into the air.

65 **PLAYING REPEATED COLLÉ BOW STROKES**—*Reset the bow after each sixteenth note.*

SOUND ADVICE

Remind students to release the bow into the air.

66   **CHANGING ENDS OF THE BOW**—*After each set of down or up bows, move to the opposite end of the bow during the rests.*

SOUND ADVICE

Remind students to release the bow into the air.

67   **CHANGING ENDS OF THE BOW ON THE D SCALE**—*After each set of down or up bows, move to the opposite end of the bow during the rests.*

SOUND ADVICE

Remind students to release the bow into the air.

Level 2: Sound Bowings
Collé

68 **PLAYING THE D SCALE USING COLLÉ**—*During the rests between sixteenth notes, lift the bow to the opposite end and prepare to play. Challenge: Reverse the bowings starting up bow at the frog and down bow at the tip.*

SOUND ADVICE

Remind students to keep the right-hand fingers active.

CRAWL COLLÉ—Divide the bow into 8 equal parts. Start at the tip, and play each stroke lower in the bow until you reach the frog. Then work back toward the tip again.

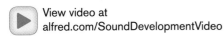 View video at
alfred.com/SoundDevelopmentVideo

VIOLIN/VIOLA

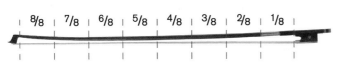

CELLO

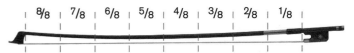

BASS

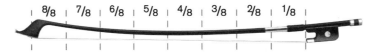

69 **LEARNING TO PLAY CRAWL COLLÉ**—*Prepare to play the* colle *stroke during the rests between notes.*

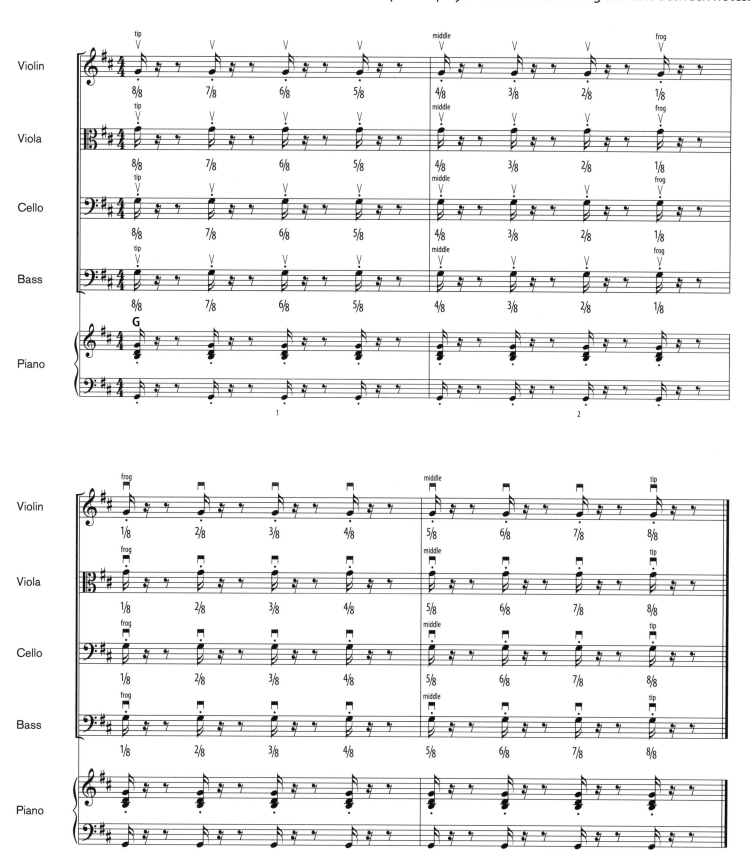

SOUND ADVICE

Remind students to divide the bow into eight equal parts.

70 **SCALE CRAWL USING COLLÉ**—*Prepare to play the* collé *stroke during the rests between notes.*

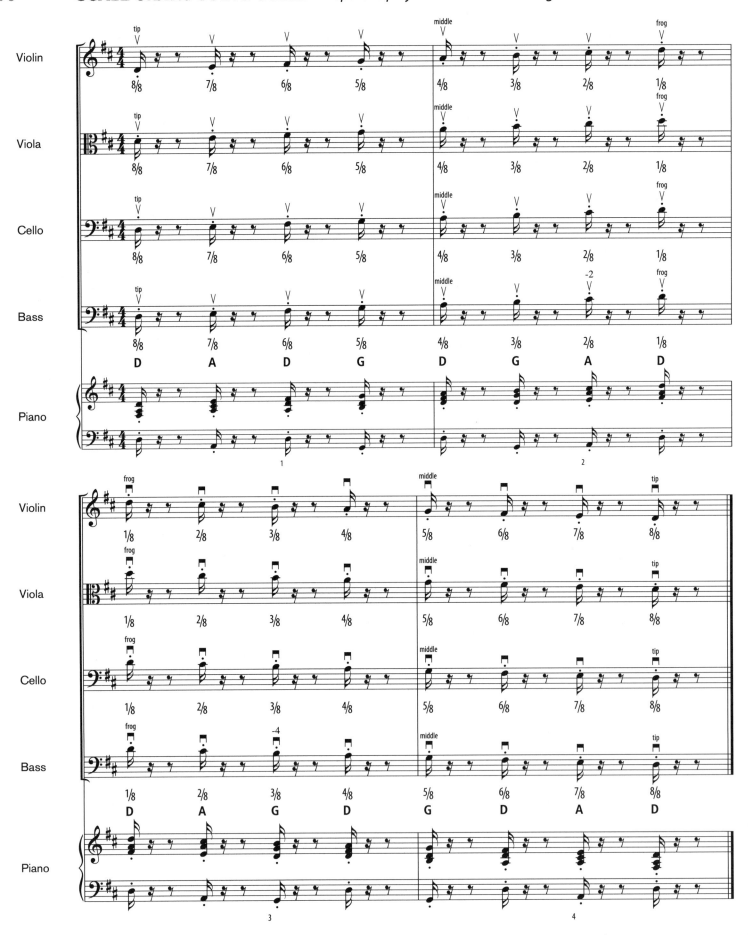

SOUND ADVICE

Remind students to divide the bow into eight equal parts.

Level 2: Sound Bowings
Spiccato

SPICCATO—Separate bow strokes that bounce off the string, sometimes called a brush stroke. *Sound Advice:* Start on the string and gradually lift weight out of the bow allowing it to bounce in an arc-like motion (⌣) over the string.

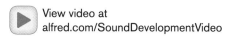 View video at
alfred.com/SoundDevelopmentVideo

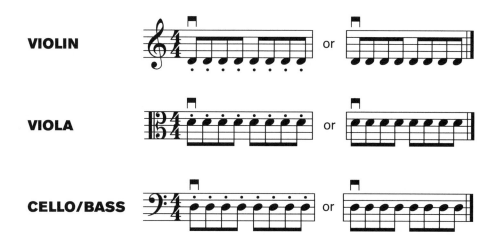

TAKING OFF—*Gradually lift weight out of the bow and shorten the stroke until the hair leaves the string and begins to bounce.*

SOUND ADVICE

Remind students to play at the balance point of the bow.

72 **LANDING**—*Gradually lengthen the stroke and add weight to the bow until the hair stays on the string.*

SOUND ADVICE

Remind students to play at the balance point of the bow.

73 **ALTERNATING ON AND OFF THE STRING**—*Practice letting the hair stay on and leave the string.*

SOUND ADVICE

Remind students to play at the balance point of the bow.

SPICCATO BOW PLACEMENTS

VIOLIN/VIOLA

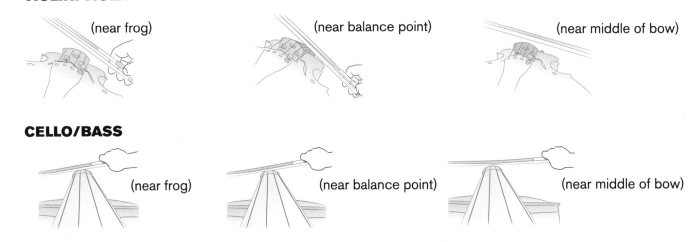

CELLO/BASS

74 **FARANDOLE**—*Practice playing* spiccato *near the frog.*

Georges Bizet

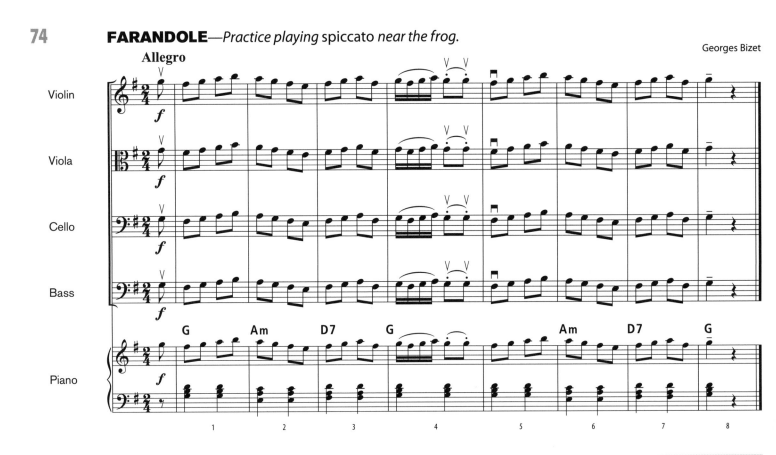

SOUND ADVICE

Remind students to play near the frog.

75 **CONTRADANSE**—*Practice playing* spiccato *at the balance point.*

Antonio Salieri

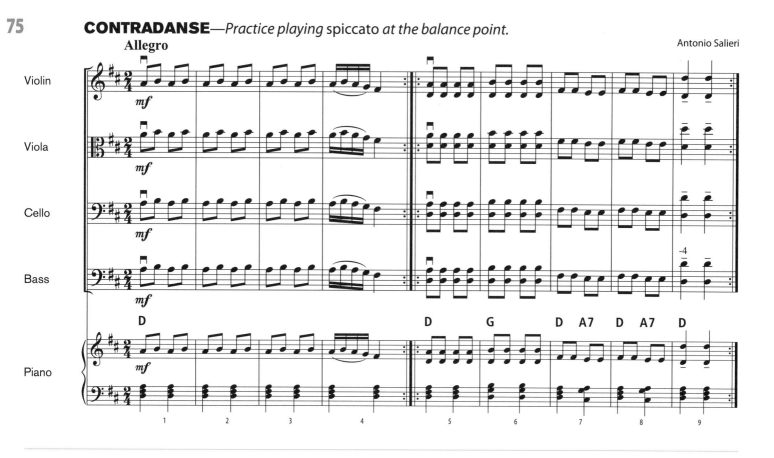

SOUND ADVICE

Remind students to play at the balance point of the bow.

76 **THE MAGIC FLUTE**—*Practice playing* spiccato *in the middle of the bow. Be careful to play the up-bow hooks with a* spiccato *bowing.*

Wolfgang Amadeus Mozart

SOUND ADVICE

Remind students to play in the middle section of the bow.

Level 2: Sound Bowings
Chop

CHOP—Indicates a percussive effect used as a rhythmic accompaniment with any number of patterns. *Sound Advice:* The down-bow chop should dig into into the string and make an additional sound on the up bow.

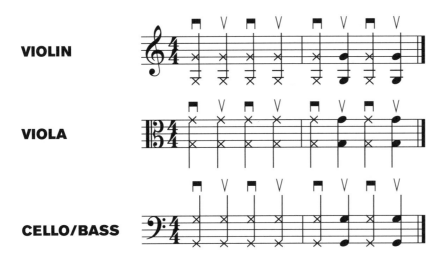

CHOPPING EXERCISE
1. Straighten your bow-hand thumb; roll the stick toward your face.
2. The bow should start close to the string.
3. Use wrist motion to slap the bow down with a slight motion toward the fingerboard (Violin/Viola) or bridge (Cello/Bass).
4. Pop the bow off the string with a slight upward motion that results in an additional sound.

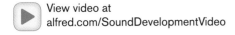 View video at
alfred.com/SoundDevelopmentVideo

77   LEARNING TO CHOP—*Using all the techniques learned above, chop on beats 2 and 4.*

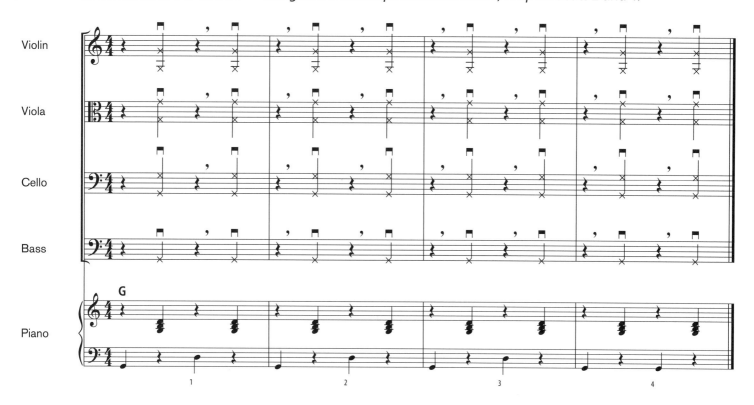

SOUND ADVICE

Remind students to play near the frog.

78   LEARNING TO CHOP AND DAMPEN—*The up-bow chop is played by flicking the bow up using your right-hand wrist and fingers. Use your left-hand fingers to dampen (d) the strings just after the up bow.*

SOUND ADVICE

Remind students to play near the frog.

79 **CHOPPING AND PLAYING**—*Practice alternating between playing chop strokes and dampened quarter notes.*

SOUND ADVICE

Remind students to play near the frog.

80 **LEARNING TO CHANGE PITCHES WHILE CHOPPING**—*Practice changing your left-hand fingers while chopping.*

SOUND ADVICE

Remind students to play near the frog.

81 **MARI'S WEDDING MELODY**—*Play the melody to* Mari's Wedding *while your stand partner plays the chop accompaniment. Take turns performing the piece in small and large ensembles with your classmates. Take turns evaluating the performances using criteria you develop with your teacher.*

Irish Fiddle Tune

SOUND ADVICE

Remind students to play in the lower half of the bow.

82 **MARI'S WEDDING CHOP ACCOMPANIMENT**—*Play the chop accompaniment to* Mari's Wedding *while your stand partner plays the melody.*

Irish Fiddle Tune

SOUND ADVICE

Remind students to play near the frog.

Level 3: Sound Shifting
Natural Harmonics

NATURAL HARMONICS occur when the string is touched lightly at the halfway point between the nut and the bridge so it vibrates on both sides of the finger. They can also occur at the point where the string is divided into three or four parts. The harmonic at the halfway point is usually notated $\frac{4}{o}$ for violins and violas and $\frac{3}{o}$ for cellos and basses.

SUL means "on the." *Sul* D indicates to play the notes on the D string.

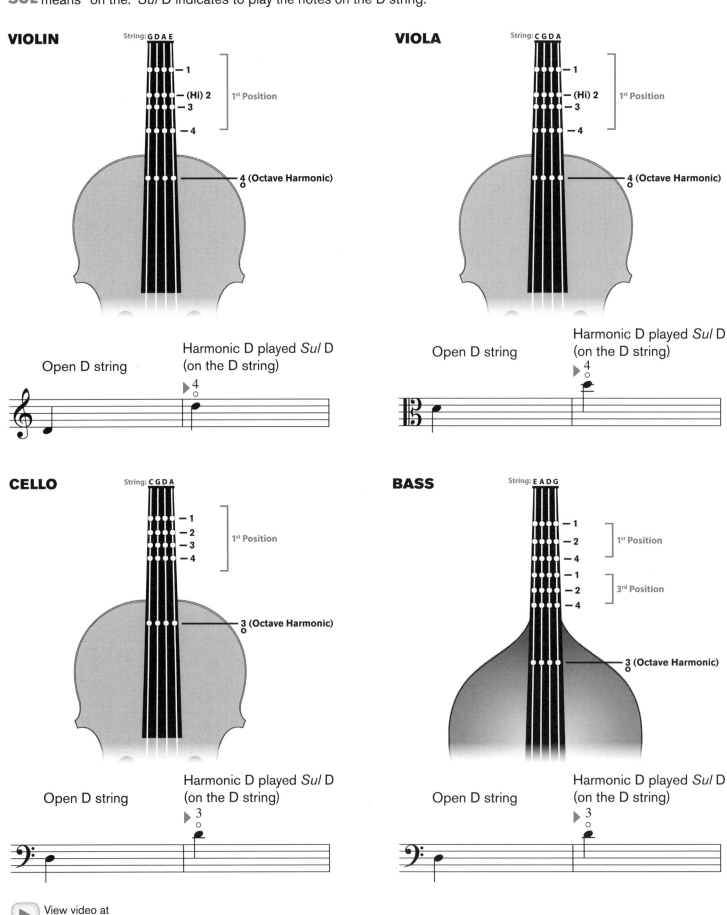

View video at
alfred.com/SoundDevelopmentVideo

83 **FINDING THE D HARMONIC**—*Be careful to follow the fingerings.*

SOUND ADVICE

Remind students to touch the string lightly when playing a harmonic.

84 **PLAYING THE D HARMONIC**—*Be careful to follow the fingerings.*

SOUND ADVICE

Remind students to touch the string lightly when playing a harmonic.

85   **PLAYING THE A HARMONIC**—*Be careful to follow the fingerings.*

SOUND ADVICE

Remind students to touch the string lightly when playing a harmonic.

86   **PLAYING THE G HARMONIC**—*Be careful to follow the fingerings.*

SOUND ADVICE

Remind students to touch the string lightly when playing a harmonic.

87 **PLAYING THE C HARMONIC**—*Violas and cellos play the C harmonic while violins and basses review.*

SOUND ADVICE

Remind students to touch the string lightly when playing a harmonic.

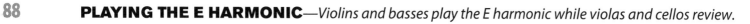

88 **PLAYING THE E HARMONIC**—*Violins and basses play the E harmonic while violas and cellos review.*

SOUND ADVICE

Remind students to touch the string lightly when playing a harmonic.

Violin Fingering Chart

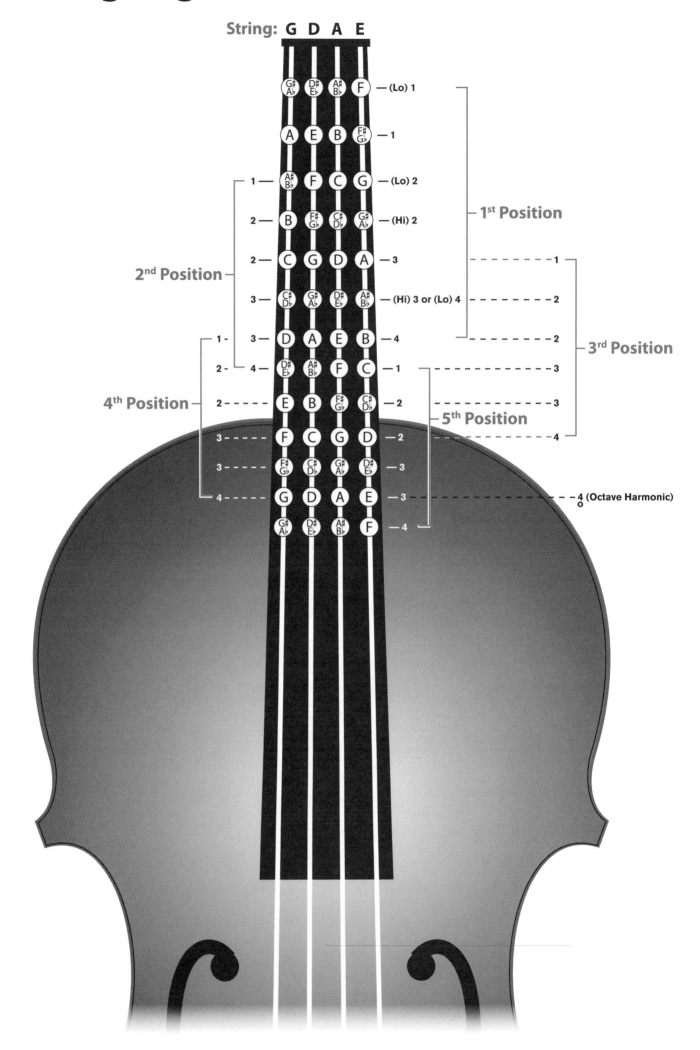

Viola Fingering Chart

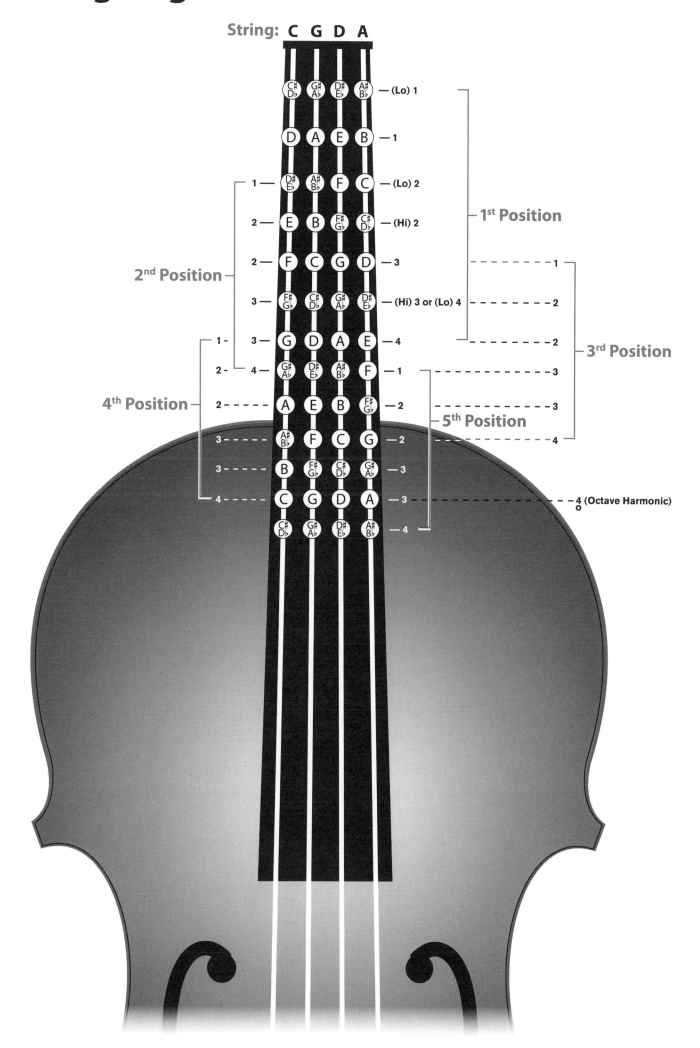

Cello Fingering Chart

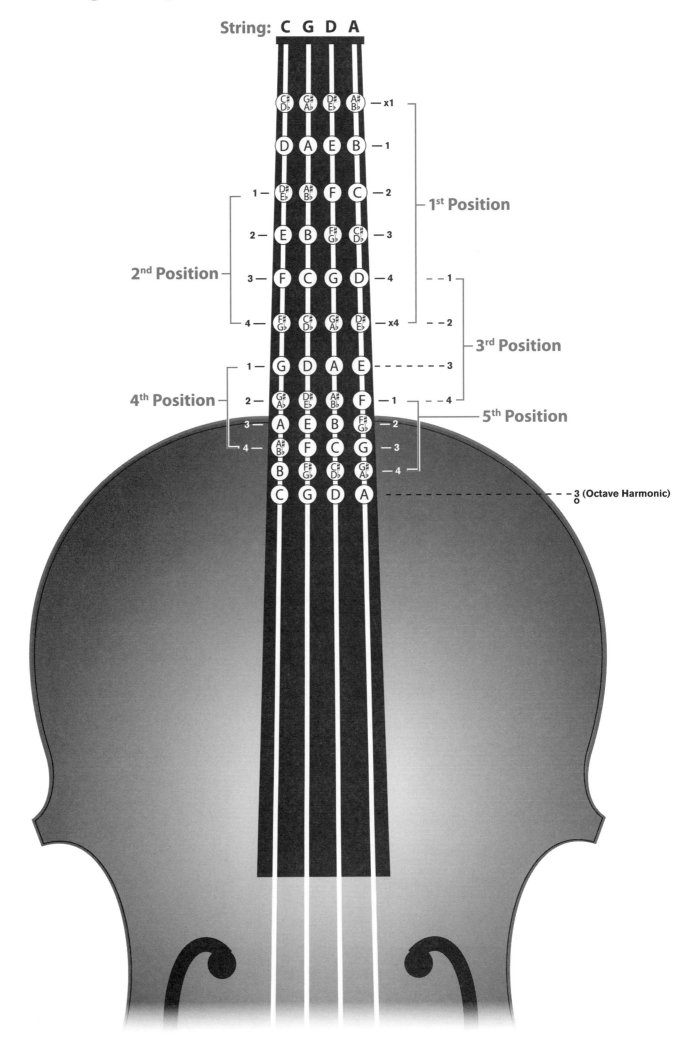

Bass Fingering Chart

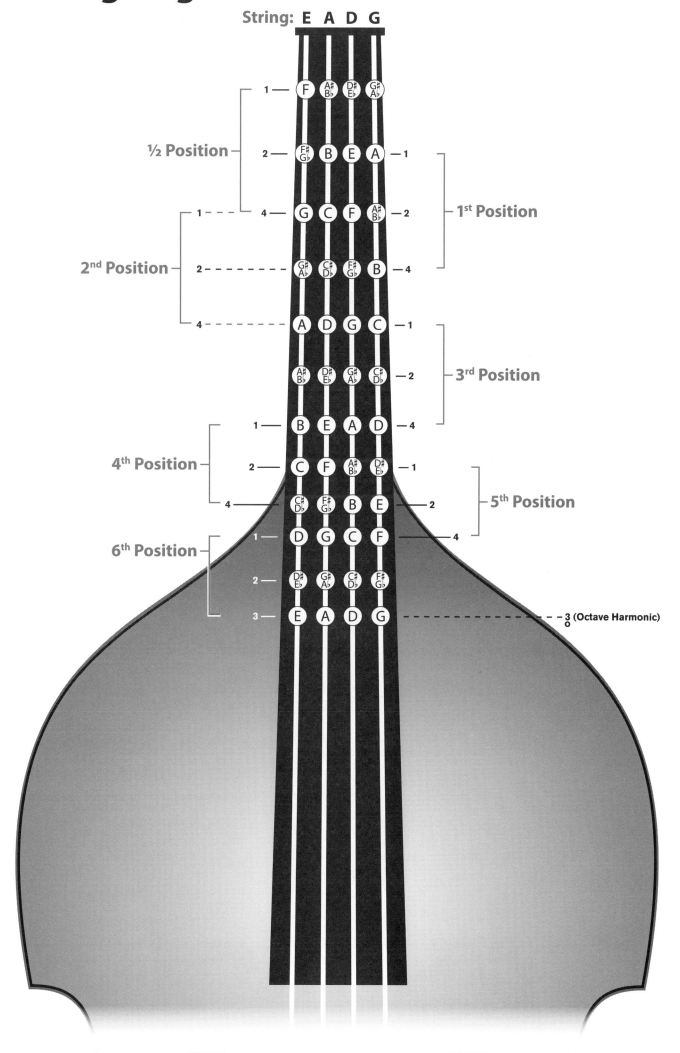

Level 3: Sound Shifting
Playing in 3rd Position: Using Pattern 1
Check your fingering chart for the new finger placements.

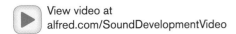 View video at
alfred.com/SoundDevelopmentVideo

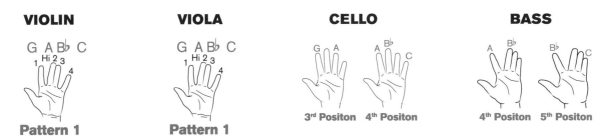

89 **FINDING 3rd POSITION ON THE D STRING USING PATTERN 1**—*Violins and violas find notes in 3rd position. Cellos find notes in 3rd and 4th positions. Basses find notes in 3rd, 4th and 5th positions.*

SOUND ADVICE

Remind students to release the left-hand thumb when shifting to a new position.

PATTERN 1 ON THE D STRING IN 3rd POSITION—*Use the fingerings as marked.*

SOUND ADVICE

Remind students to follow all fingerings.

91   **PATTERN 1 ON THE D STRING IN 3rd POSITION AGAIN**—*Use the fingerings as marked.*

Basses play on the D and G strings.

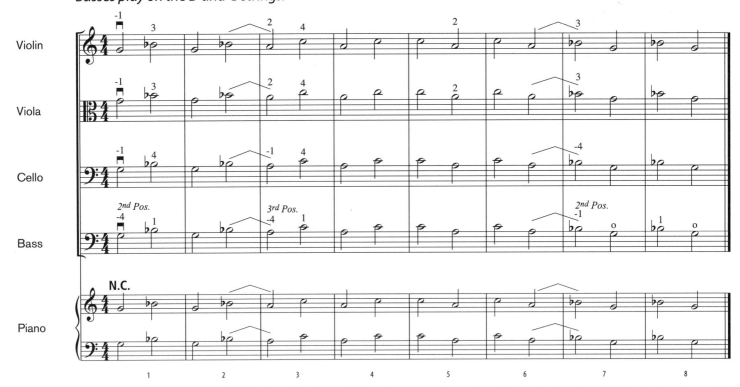

SOUND ADVICE

Remind students to follow all fingerings.

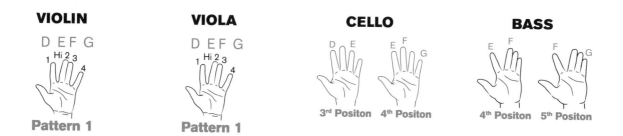

92

FINDING 3rd POSITION ON THE A STRING USING PATTERN 1—*Violins and violas find notes in 3rd position. Cellos find notes in 3rd and 4th positions. Basses find notes in 3rd, 4th and 5th positions.*

SOUND ADVICE

Remind students to release the left-hand thumb when shifting to a new position.

93 **PATTERN 1 ON THE A STRING IN 3rd POSITION**—*Use the fingerings as marked.*

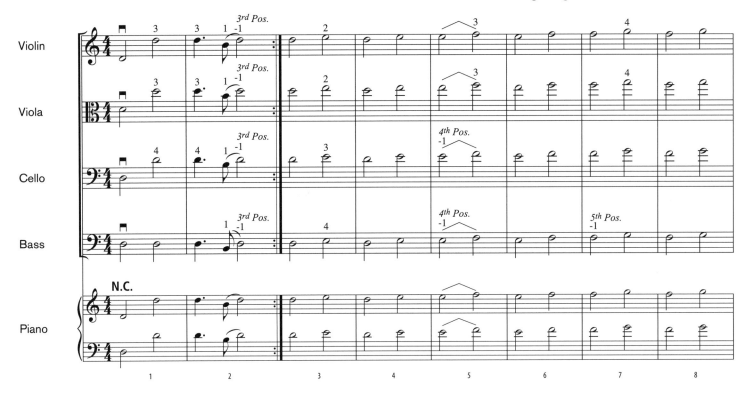

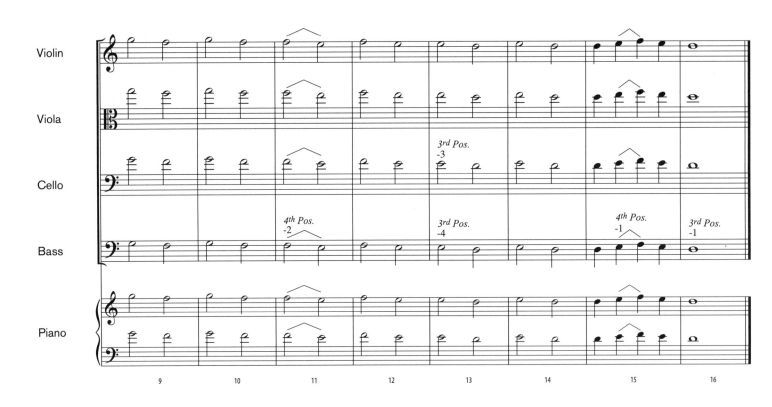

SOUND ADVICE

Remind students to follow all fingerings.

94 **PATTERN 1 ON THE A STRING IN 3rd POSITION AGAIN**—*Use the fingerings as marked. Basses play on the A and D strings.*

SOUND ADVICE

Remind students to follow all fingerings.

Level 3: Sound Shifting
Playing in 3rd Position: Using Pattern 1
Check your fingering chart for the new finger placements.

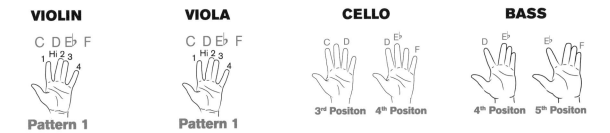

95 **FINDING 3rd POSITION ON THE G STRING USING PATTERN 1**—*Violins and violas find notes in 3rd position. Cellos find notes in 3rd and 4th positions. Basses find notes in 3rd, 4th and 5th positions.*

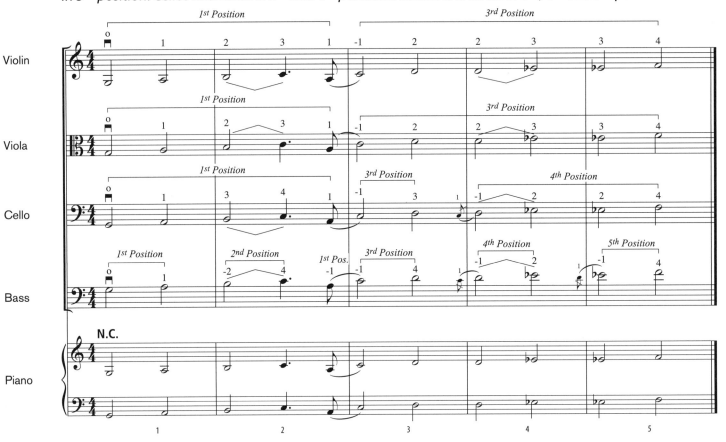

SOUND ADVICE

Remind the students to release the left-hand thumb when shifting to a new position.

96 **PATTERN 1 ON THE G STRING IN 3rd POSITION**—*Use the fingerings as marked.*

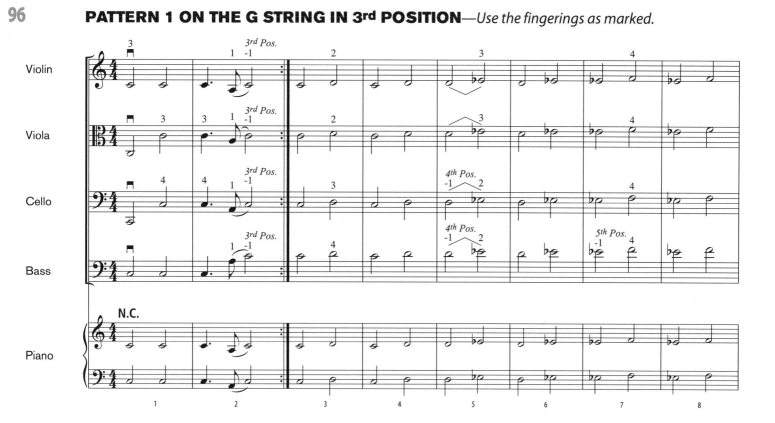

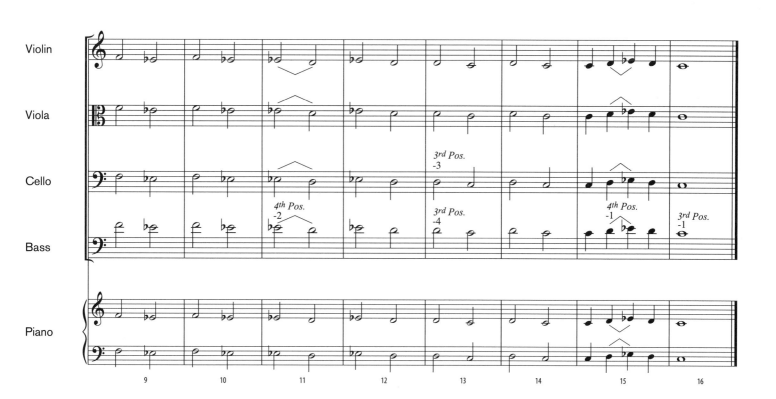

SOUND ADVICE

Remind the students to follow all fingerings.

97 **PATTERN 1 ON THE G STRING IN 3rd POSITION AGAIN**—*Use the fingerings as marked.*
Basses play on the A and D strings.

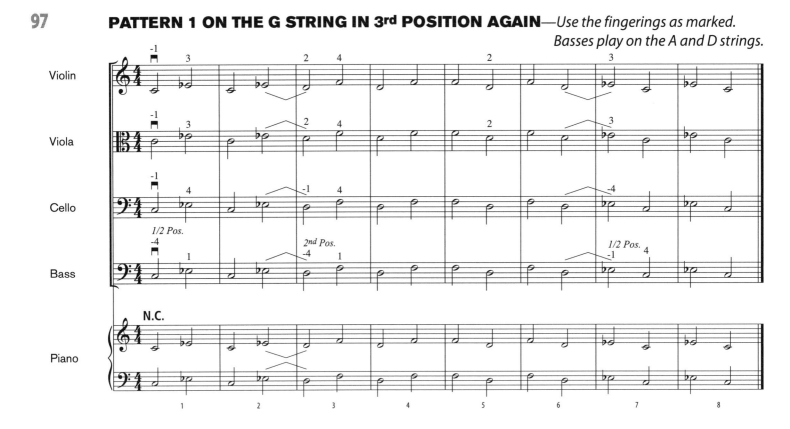

SOUND ADVICE

Remind the students to follow all fingerings.

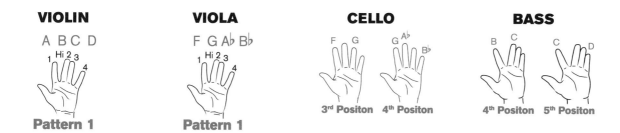

98

FINDING 3rd POSITION ON THE E AND C STRINGS USING PATTERN 1—*Violins and violas find notes in 3rd position. Cellos find notes in 3rd and 4th positions. Basses find notes in 3rd, 4th and 5th positions.*

SOUND ADVICE

Remind the students to release the left-hand thumb when shifting to a new position.

99 **PATTERN 1 ON THE E AND C STRINGS IN 3rd POSITION**—*Use the fingerings as marked.*

SOUND ADVICE

Remind the students to follow all fingerings.

PATTERN 1 ON THE E AND C STRINGS IN
3rd POSITION AGAIN—*Use the fingerings as marked. Basses play on the A and D strings.*

SOUND ADVICE

Remind students to follow all fingerings.

Level 3: Sound Shifting
Playing in 3rd Position: Using Pattern 1

101   **LAS MAÑANITAS**—*Play* Las Mañanitas *in 3rd position using Pattern No. 1. Cellos and basses play in a variety of positions. Perform this piece for your friends and family using good left and right hand technique.*

Mexican Birthday Song

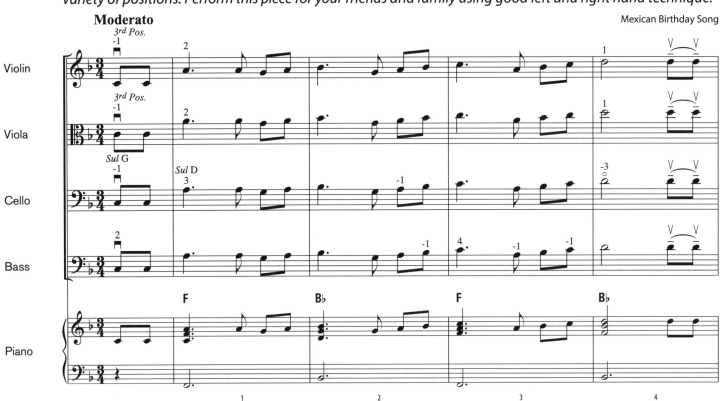

SOUND ADVICE

Remind students to keep the left hand relaxed.

102 **CHESTER**—*Play* Chester *in 3rd position using Pattern No. 1. Cellos and basses play in a variety of positions. Challenge: Take turns performing* Chester *for your classmates. While listening, practice good concert etiquette.*

William Billings

SOUND ADVICE

Remind students to keep the left hand relaxed.

Level 3: Sound Shifting
Shifting from 1ˢᵗ to 3ʳᵈ Position

A **GUIDE/TRANSPORT FINGER** is the finger you use to shift from one position to another. It helps guide/transport you to the new position. *Sound Advice:* Just before the guide/transport finger is ready to move to the new position, release the weight in the finger as if you are playing a harmonic. Then smoothly move to the new position and reapply the finger weight.

103 **SHIFTING FROM 1ˢᵗ TO 3ʳᵈ POSITION**—*Violins and violas practice shifting from 1ˢᵗ to 3ʳᵈ position. Cellos and basses play in a variety of positions.*

SOUND ADVICE

Remind students to follow all fingerings.

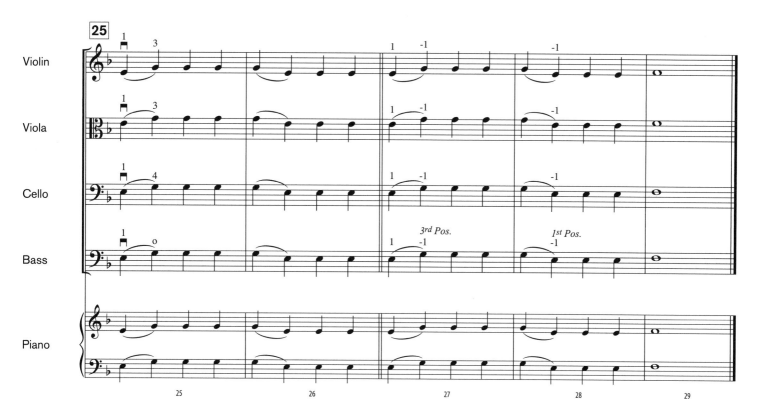

Level 3: Sound Shifting
Playing in 3rd Position: Using Pattern 2
Check your fingering chart for the new finger placements.

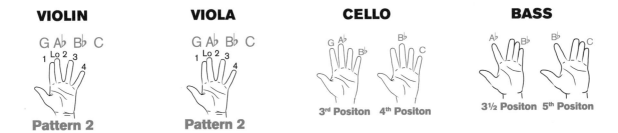

104 **FINDING 3rd POSITION ON THE D STRING USING PATTERN 2**—*Violins and violas find notes in 3rd position. Cellos find notes in 3rd and 4th positions. Basses find notes in 3rd, 3 1/2 and 5th positions.*

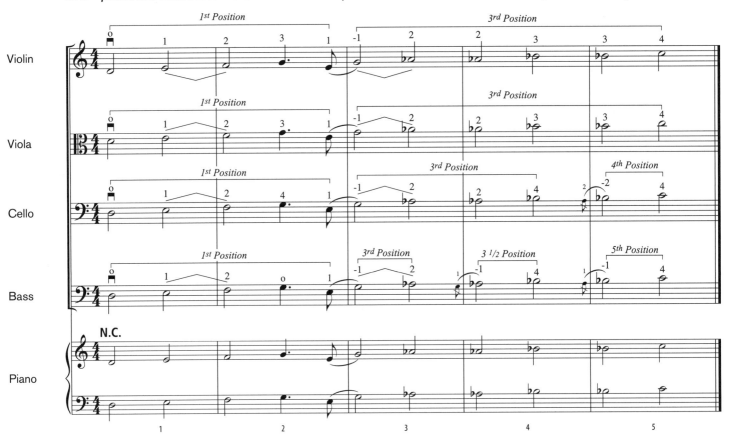

SOUND ADVICE

Remind students to release the left-hand thumb when shifting to a new position.

PATTERN 2 ON THE D STRING IN 3rd POSITION—*Use the fingerings as marked. Cellos and basses play in a variety of positions.*

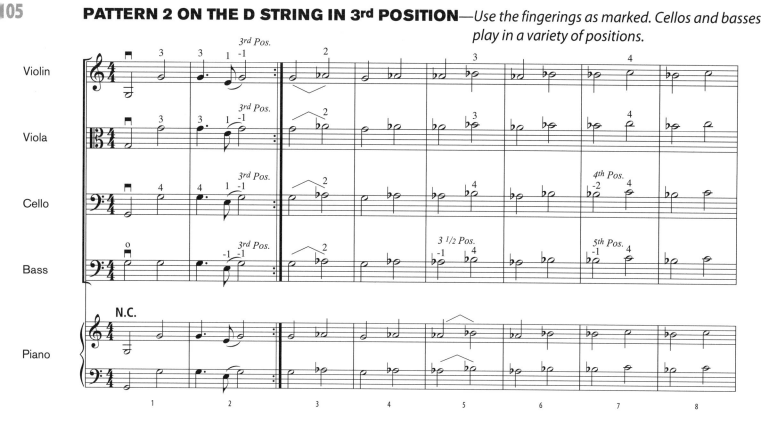

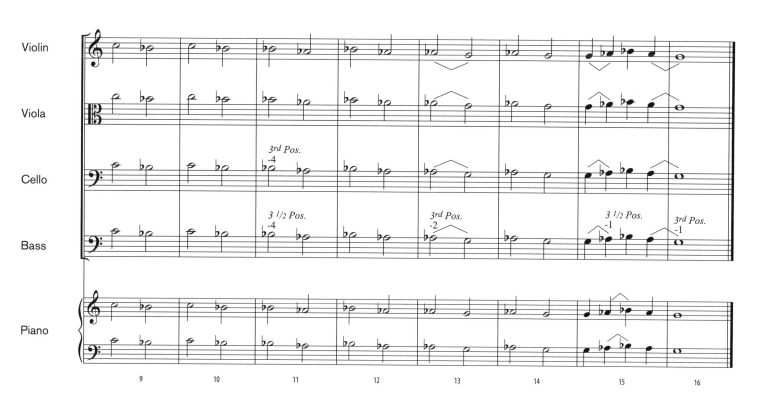

SOUND ADVICE

Remind students to follow all fingerings.

106

PATTERN 2 ON THE D STRING IN
3rd POSITION AGAIN—*Use the fingerings as marked. Cellos and basses play in a variety of positions.*

SOUND ADVICE

Remind students to follow all fingerings.

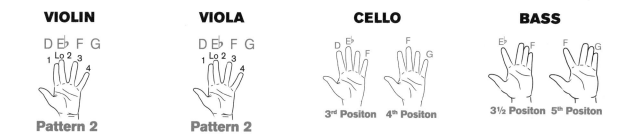

107

FINDING 3rd POSITION ON THE A STRING USING PATTERN 2—*Violins and violas find notes in 3rd position. Cellos find notes in 3rd and 4th positions. Basses find notes in 3rd, 3 1/2 and 5th positions.*

SOUND ADVICE

Remind students to release the left-hand thumb when shifting to a new position.

108 **PATTERN 2 ON THE A STRING IN 3rd POSITION**—*Use the fingerings as marked. Cellos and basses play in a variety of positions.*

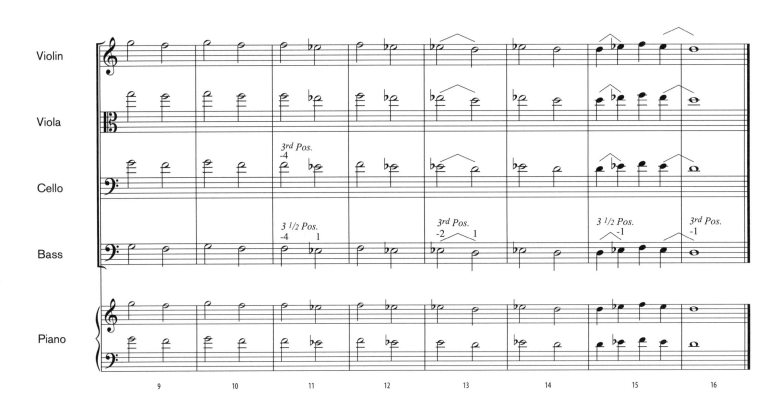

SOUND ADVICE

Remind the students to follow all fingerings.

PATTERN 2 ON THE A STRING IN 3rd POSITION AGAIN—*Use the fingerings as marked.*
Cellos and basses play in a variety of positions.

SOUND ADVICE

Remind students to follow all fingerings.

Level 3: Sound Shifting
Playing in 3rd Position: Using Pattern 2
Check your fingering chart for the new finger placements.

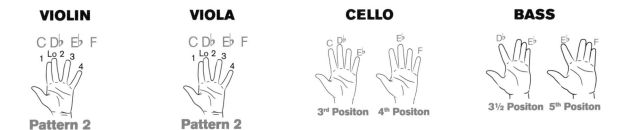

110 **FINDING 3rd POSITION ON THE G STRING USING PATTERN 2**—*Violins and violas find notes in 3rd position. Cellos find notes in 3rd and 4th positions. Basses find notes in 3rd, 3 1/2 and 5th positions.*

SOUND ADVICE

Remind students to release the left-hand thumb when shifting to a new position.

11   **PATTERN 2 ON THE G STRING IN 3rd POSITION**—*Use the fingerings as marked.*

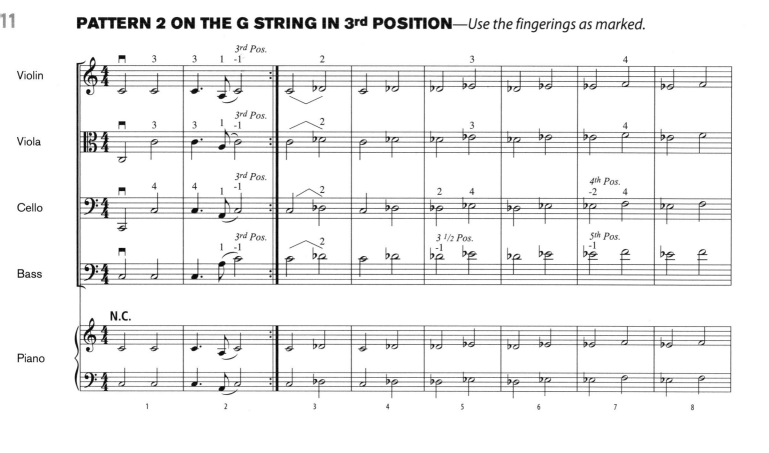

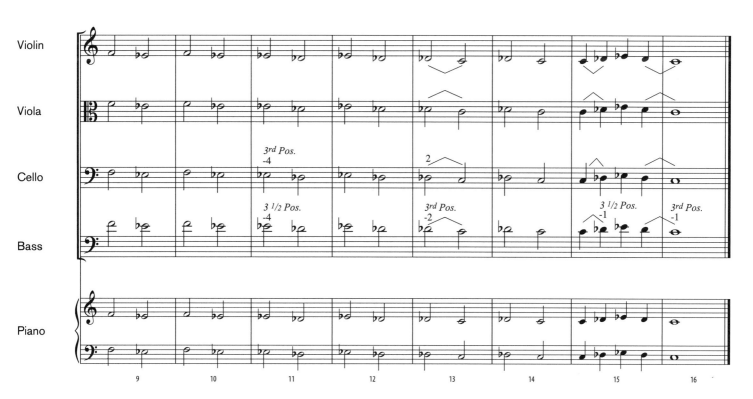

SOUND ADVICE

Remind students to follow all fingerings.

110

112 PATTERN 2 ON THE G STRING IN 3rd POSITION AGAIN—*Use the fingerings as marked.*
Basses review.

SOUND ADVICE

Remind students to follow all fingerings.

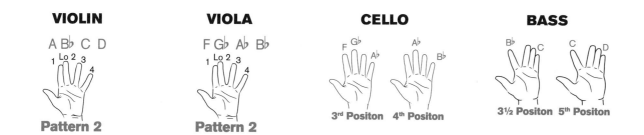

113

FINDING 3rd POSITION ON THE E AND C STRINGS USING PATTERN 2—*Violins and violas find notes in 3rd position. Cellos find notes in 3rd and 4th positions. Basses find notes in 3rd, 3 1/2 and 5th positions.*

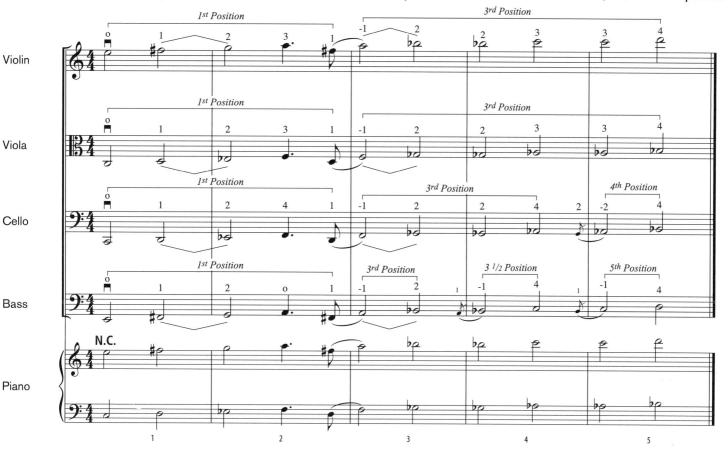

SOUND ADVICE

Remind students to release the left-hand thumb when shifting to a new position.

112

114 **PATTERN 2 ON THE E AND C STRING IN 3rd POSITION**—*Use the fingerings as marked.*

Cellos and basses play in a variety of positions.

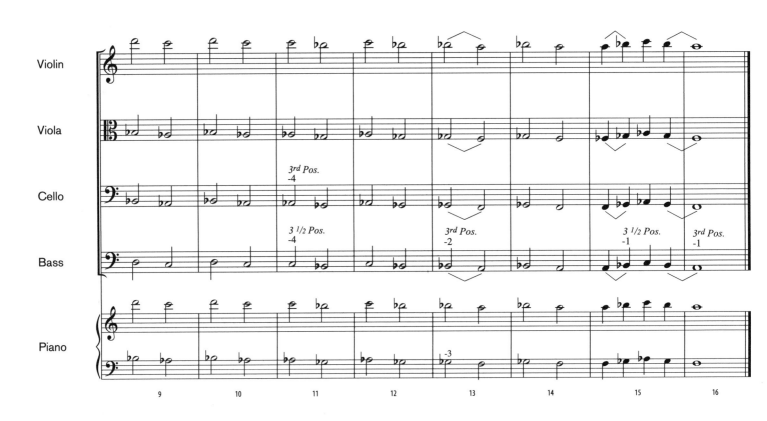

SOUND ADVICE

Remind the students to follow all fingerings.

PATTERN 2 ON THE E AND C STRINGS IN 3rd POSITION AGAIN—*Use the fingerings as marked.*

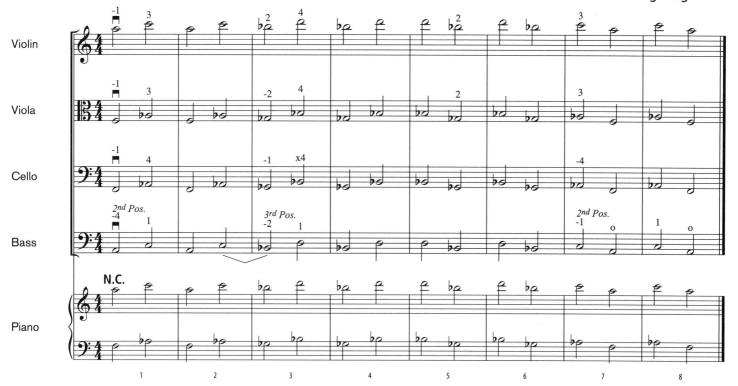

SOUND ADVICE

Remind students to follow all fingerings.

Level 3: Sound Shifting
Playing in 3ʳᵈ Position: Using Pattern 3
Check your fingering chart for the new finger placements.

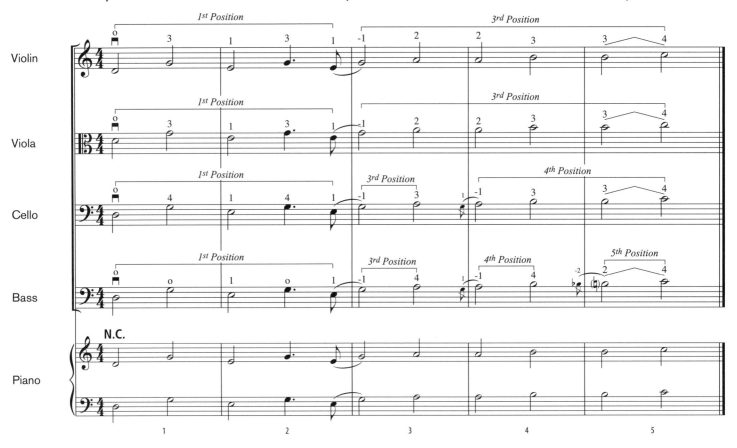

116   **FINDING 3ʳᵈ POSITION ON THE D STRING USING PATTERN 3**—*Violins and violas find notes in 3ʳᵈ position. Cellos find notes in 3ʳᵈ and 4ᵗʰ positions. Basses find notes in 3ʳᵈ, 4ᵗʰ and 5ᵗʰ positions.*

SOUND ADVICE

Remind students to release the left-hand thumb when shifting to a new position.

117 **PATTERN 3 ON THE D STRING IN 3rd POSITION**—*Use the fingerings as marked.*

SOUND ADVICE

Remind students to follow all fingerings.

118 **PATTERN 3 ON THE D STRING IN 3rd POSITION AGAIN**—*Use the fingerings as marked.*

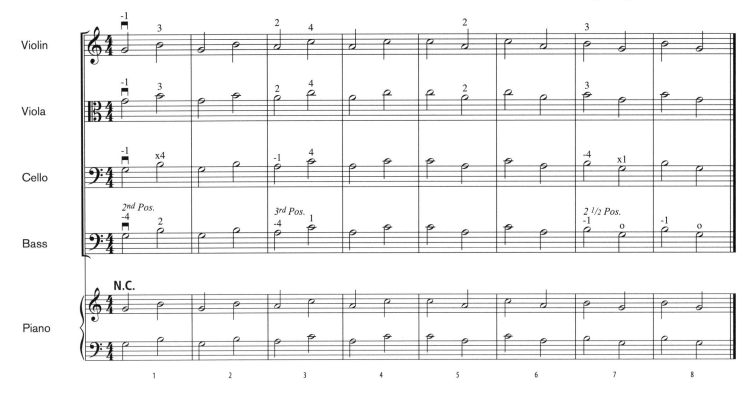

SOUND ADVICE

Remind students to follow all fingerings.

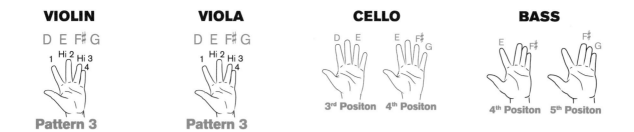

19

FINDING 3rd POSITION ON THE A STRING USING PATTERN 3—*Violins and violas find notes in 3rd position. Cellos find notes in 3rd and 4th positions. Basses find notes in 3rd, 4th and 5th positions.*

SOUND ADVICE

Remind students to release the left-hand thumb when shifting to a new position.

120 **PATTERN 3 ON THE A STRING IN 3rd POSITION**—*Use the fingerings as marked.*

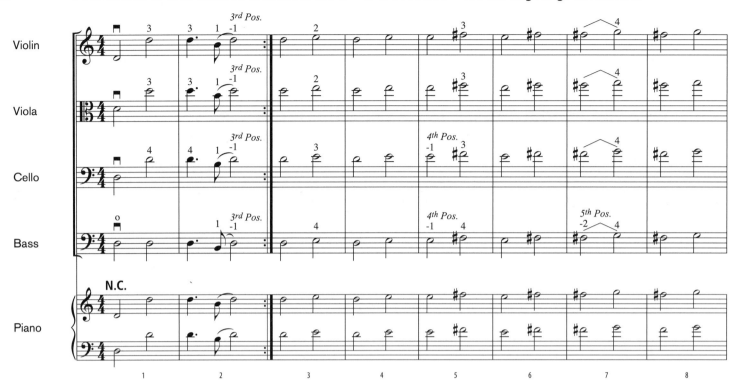

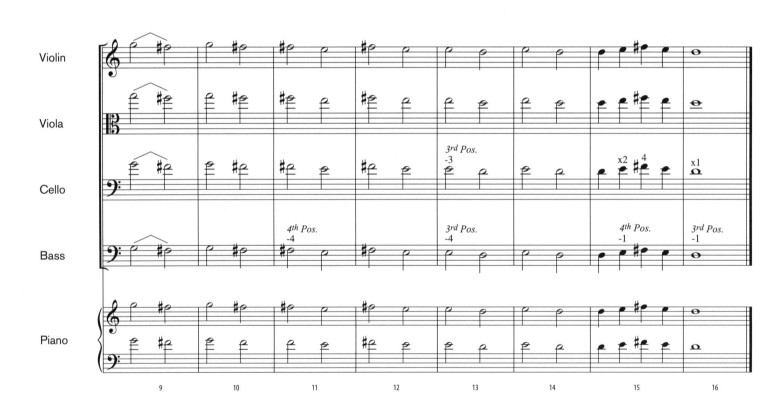

SOUND ADVICE

Remind the students to follow all fingerings.

121 ## PATTERN 3 ON THE A STRING IN 3rd POSITION AGAIN—*Use the fingerings as marked.*

SOUND ADVICE

Remind students to follow all fingerings.

Level 3: Sound Shifting
Playing in 3rd Position: Using Pattern 3
Check your fingering chart for the new finger placements.

122   **FINDING 3rd POSITION ON THE G STRING USING PATTERN 3**—*Violins and violas find notes in 3rd position. Cellos find notes in 3rd and 4th positions. Basses find notes in 3rd, 4th and 5th positions.*

SOUND ADVICE
Remind students to release the left-hand thumb when shifting to a new position.

123 **PATTERN 3 ON THE G STRING IN 3rd POSITION**—*Use the fingerings as marked.*

SOUND ADVICE

Remind students to follow all fingerings.

124 **PATTERN 3 ON THE G STRING IN 3rd POSITION AGAIN**—*Use the fingerings as marked.*

SOUND ADVICE

Remind students to follow all fingerings.

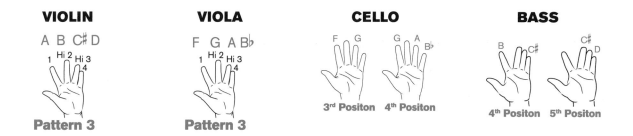

FINDING 3rd POSITION ON THE E AND C STRINGS USING PATTERN 3—*Violins and violas find notes in 3rd position. Cellos find notes in 3rd and 4th positions. Basses find notes in 3rd, 4th and 5th positions.*

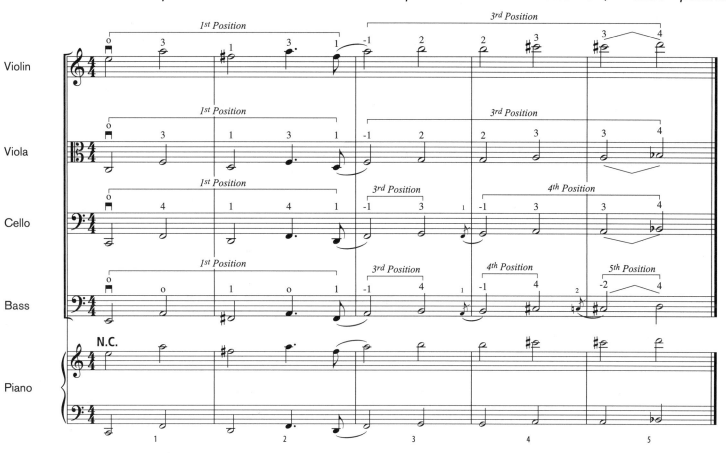

SOUND ADVICE

Remind students to release the left-hand thumb when shifting to a new position.

124

126 **PATTERN 3 ON THE E AND C STRINGS IN 3rd POSITION**—*Use the fingerings as marked.*

SOUND ADVICE

Remind the students to follow all fingerings.

27 **PATTERN 3 ON THE E AND C STRINGS IN 3rd POSITION AGAIN**—*Use the fingerings as marked.*

SOUND ADVICE

Remind students to follow all fingerings.

Level 3: Sound Shifting
Playing in 3rd Position: Using Pattern 2

128 **THEME FROM VIOLIN CONCERTO**—*Violins and violas play* Theme from Violin Concerto *in 3rd position using Pattern No. 2. Cellos use 3rd and 4th positions. Basses use 2nd and 3 1/2 positions.*

Allegro ma troppo

Ludwig van Beethoven

SOUND ADVICE

Remind the students to follow all fingerings.

MARCH FROM JUDAS MACCABEUS—*Violins and violas play* Judas Maccabeus *in 3rd position using Pattern No. 2. Cellos use 3rd and 4th positions. Basses use 2nd and 3 1/2 positions.*

George Frideric Handel

SOUND ADVICE

Remind the students to follow all fingerings.

130 **AURA LEE**—*Violins and violas play* Aura Lee *in 3rd position using Pattern No. 2. Before playing, mark the half steps using (⌄). Cellos use 3rd and 4th positions. Basses use 3rd, 4th and 5th positions.*
Challenge: Listen to a recording of this song and identify the number of sections. After playing the piece, circle the sections that are alike.

George R. Poulton

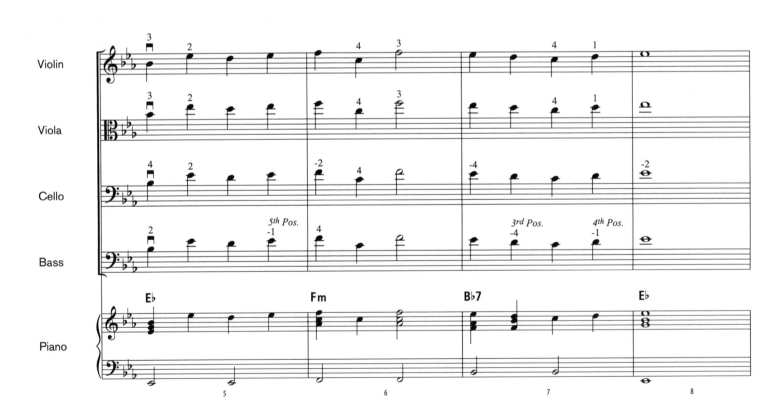

SOUND ADVICE

Remind the students to follow all fingerings.

Level 3: Sound Shifting
Shifting from 1st to 3rd Position

131   **LONG, LONG AGO**—*Violins and violas practice going from 1st to 3rd position. Cellos practice 3rd and 4th positions. Basses practice 2nd, 3rd and 4th positions. Challenge: Play* Long, Long Ago *from memory.*

Thomas Haynes Bayly

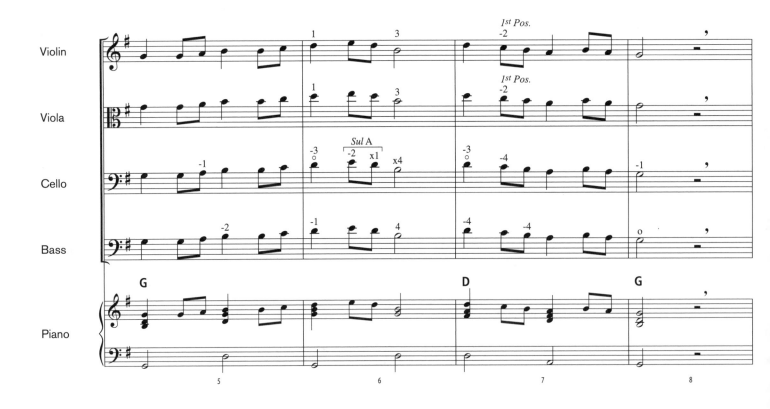

SOUND ADVICE

Remind the students to follow all fingerings.

132 **SCOTTISH AIR**—*Violins and violas practice going from 1st to 3rd position. Cellos practice 3rd and 4th positions. Basses practice 2nd, 3rd, 4th and 5th positions. Challenge: Use all the sound variables from Level 1 to play Scottish Air expressively.*

Traditional

SOUND ADVICE

Remind the students to follow all fingerings.

Level 3: Sound Shifting
Playing In 3rd Position: Using Pattern 3

Check your fingering chart for the new finger placements.

133 **THEME FROM SERENADE FOR STRINGS**—*Violins and violas play* Theme from Serenade for String
in 3rd position using Pattern No. 3. Cellos play in 3rd and 4th positions. Basses play in 2nd, 3rd, 4th and 5th position

Pyotr Ilyich Tchaikovsky

SOUND ADVICE

Remind the students to follow all fingerings.

THEME FROM SYMPHONY No. 9—*Violins and violas play* Theme from Symphony No. 9 *in 3rd position using Pattern No. 3. Cellos play in 3rd position. Basses play in 3rd and 4th positions.*

Antonín Dvořák

SOUND ADVICE

Remind the students to follow all fingerings.

135   **THEME FROM ROSAMUNDE**—*Violins and violas play* Theme from Rosamunde *in 3rd position using Pattern No. 3. Cellos play in 3rd and 4th positions. Basses play in 3rd, 4th and 5th positions.*

Franz Schubert

SOUND ADVICE

Remind the students to follow all fingerings.

ALLELUIA—*Violins and violas play* Alleluia *in 3rd position using Pattern No. 3. Cellos play in 3rd and 4th positions. Basses play in 3rd, 4th and 5th positions.*

Wolfgang Amadeus Mozart

SOUND ADVICE

Remind the students to follow all fingerings.

Level 3: Sound Shifting
Playing In 2ⁿᵈ Position: Using Pattern 3

Check your fingering chart for the new finger placements.

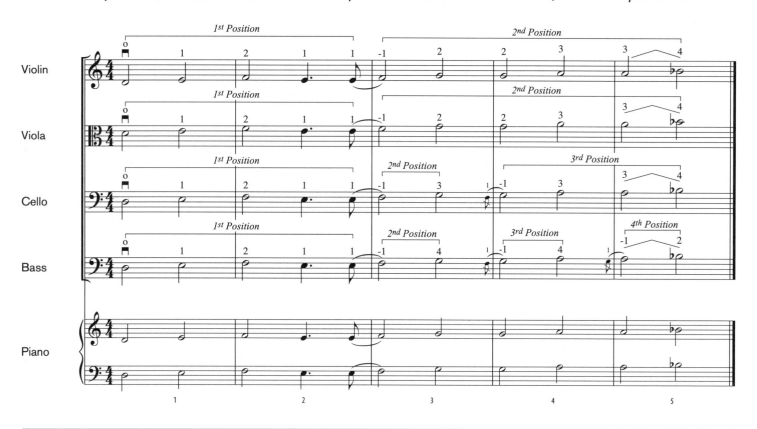

137   **FINDING 2nd POSITION ON THE D STRING USING PATTERN 3**—*Violins and violas find notes 2ⁿᵈ position. Cellos find notes in 2ⁿᵈ and 3ʳᵈ positions. Basses find notes in 2ⁿᵈ, 3ʳᵈ and 4ᵗʰ positions.*

SOUND ADVICE

Remind students to release the left-hand thumb when shifting to a new position.

MORE PLAYING IN 2nd POSITION—*Be careful to follow all fingerings.*

SOUND ADVICE

Remind the students to follow all fingerings.

139 **MATTACHINS (SWORD DANCE)**—*Play* Sword Dance *using 2nd position.*

Renaissance Dance

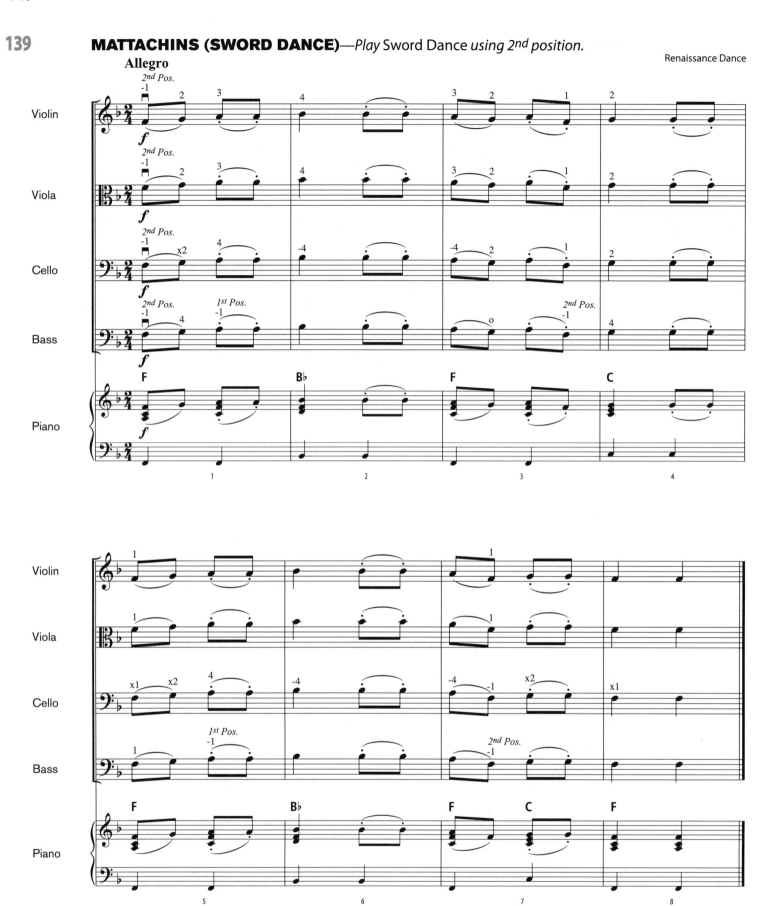

SOUND ADVICE

Remind the students to follow all fingerings.

ETUDE—*Write the fingerings over each note that can be played in 2nd position.*

Charles de Beriot

SOUND ADVICE

Remind the students to follow all fingerings.

Level 3: Sound Shifting
Playing In 4ᵗʰ Position: Using Pattern 1

Check your fingering chart for the new finger placements.

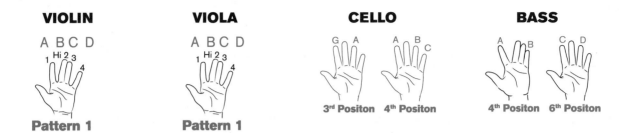

141 **FINDING 4ᵗʰ POSITION ON THE D STRING USING PATTERN No. 1**—*Practice finding 4ᵗʰ position. Basses play in 4ᵗʰ and 6ᵗʰ positions.*

SOUND ADVICE

Remind students to release the left-hand thumb when shifting to a new position.

42 ## LEARNING TO PLAY IN 4th POSITION—*Learn to play in 4th position. Basses play in 4th, 5th and 6th positions.*

SOUND ADVICE

Remind the students to follow all fingerings.

143   **PERPETUAL MOTION IN 4th POSITION**—*Be careful to follow all fingerings. Cellos and basses review.*
Challenge: Write in the remaining fingerings.

Traditional

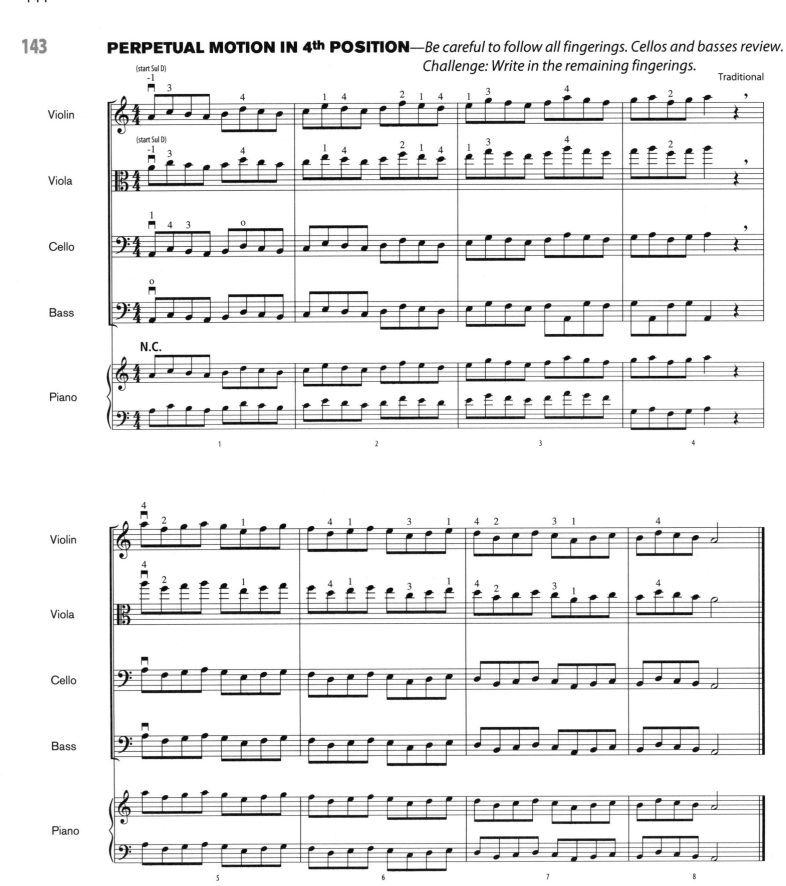

SOUND ADVICE

Remind the students to follow all fingerings.

44 **PLAYING IN 4th POSITION**—*Practice playing in 4th position. Basses play in 4th, 5th and 6th positions.*

SOUND ADVICE

Remind the students to follow all fingerings.

Level 3: Sound Shifting
Playing In 5th Position: Using Pattern 3

Check your fingering chart for the new finger placements.

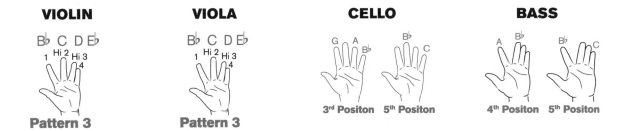

145   **FINDING 5th POSITION ON THE D STRING USING PATTERN No. 3**—*Practice finding 5th positi*

SOUND ADVICE

Remind students to release the left-hand thumb when shifting to a new position.

5th POSITION ON THE D STRING—*Violin and viola 5th position fingerings can be read as if they were in 1st position one string higher.*

SOUND ADVICE

Remind the students to follow all fingerings.

147   5th POSITION ON THE A STRING—*Violin and viola 5th position fingerings can be read as if they were in 1st position one string higher. Cellos and basses review.*

SOUND ADVICE

Remind the students to follow all fingerings.

Level 3: Sound Shifting
Playing In 5th Position: Using Pattern 3

Check your fingering chart for the new finger placements.

5th POSITION ON THE VIOLIN E STRING—*Violin 5th position fingerings can be read as if they were in 1st position one string higher. Violas and cellos review.*

SOUND ADVICE

Remind the students to follow all fingerings.

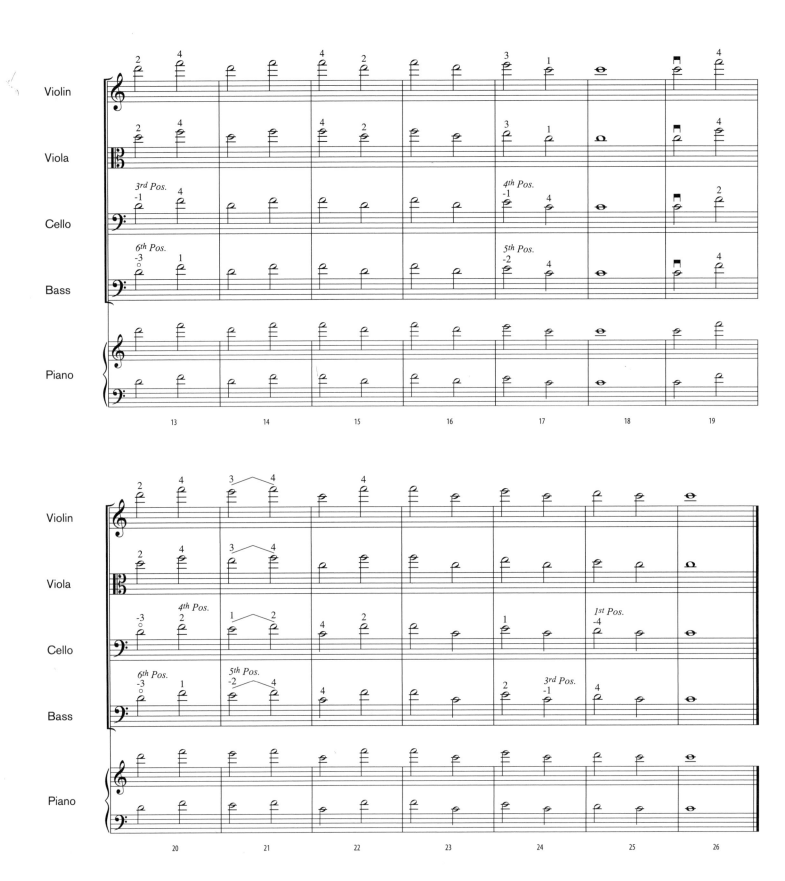

149 **5th POSITION WORKOUT**—*Practice playing in 5th position on the D and A strings. Cellos and basses review.*

SOUND ADVICE

Remind the students to follow all fingerings.

Level 3: Sound Shifting
Shifting from 3rd to 5th Position

150 **SHIFTING FROM 3rd TO 5th POSITION ON THE A STRING**—*Be careful to follow all fingerings.*

Violins and violas practice going from 3rd to 5th position. Cellos and basses reveiw.

SOUND ADVICE

Remind the students to follow all fingerings.

51 **SHIFTING FROM 3rd TO 5th POSITION ON THE VIOLIN E STRING**—*Be careful to follow all fingerings. Violins practice going from 3rd to 5th position. Violas, cellos and basses reveiw.*

SOUND ADVICE

Remind the students to follow all fingerings.

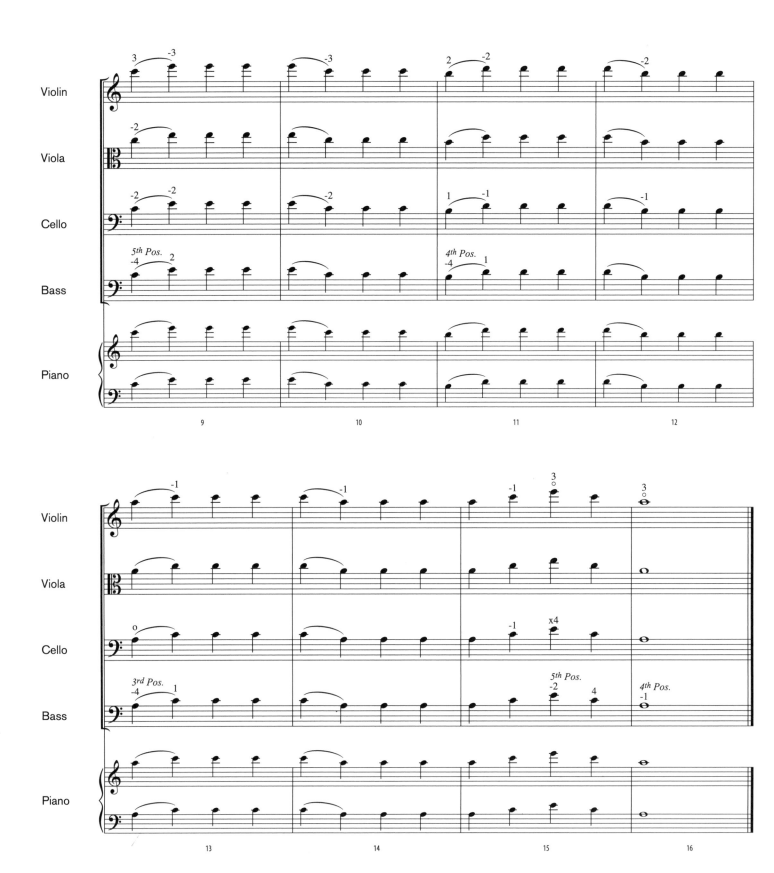

Level 3: Sound Shifting
Vibrato

PREPARING FOR VIBRATO

1. **FINGER ROCKERS**—Place your left-hand 2nd finger in the channel between your 3rd and 4th finger bones. Gently rock your finger up and down your hand.

2. **FINGER SHOOTS**—While holding the violin in guitar position lightly place your left-hand 2nd finger on the D string. Move up and down the string as if you are wiping off the dust. Gradually go faster and faster from 1st position to the top of the fingerboard. Now repeat in shoulder position.

BOUT VIBRATO

3. **ARM VIBRATO**—Hold the violin in guitar position. Place your right hand on the bout and then slide your left hand up the D string until it touches your right hand. Place your 2nd finger on the D string. Remove your right hand. Starting the motion from your left forearm gently rock your 2nd finger up and down the string so your left hand bounces off the bout. Now repeat in shoulder position.

4. **HAND VIBRATO**—Hold the violin in guitar position. Slide your left hand up the D string until it touches the bout. Gently rock your 2nd finger up and down the string and keep your hand in contact with the bout. Now repeat in shoulder position.

VIOLIN

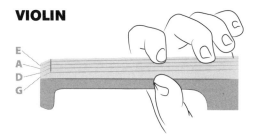

VIOLA

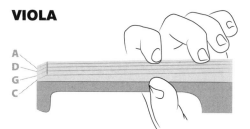

CELLO

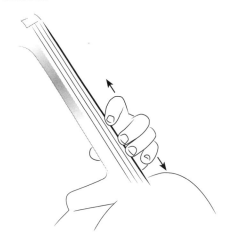

BASS

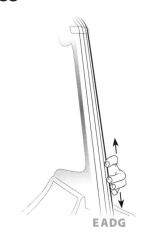

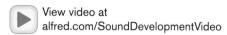

View video at
alfred.com/SoundDevelopmentVideo

VIBRATO is a slight fluctuation of the pitch below and above the written note. The vibrato finger rocks back and forth rapidly around the center point of the pitch to create a beautiful sound. The left hand will look like it shakes back and forth. Vibrato will warm the sound.

ROLLING THE FINGER BACKWARD–Gently roll the finger from the A to slightly below the A.

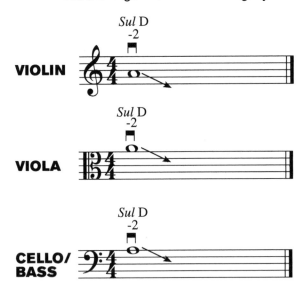

ROLLING THE FINGER FORWARD–Gently roll the finger from the A to slightly above the A.

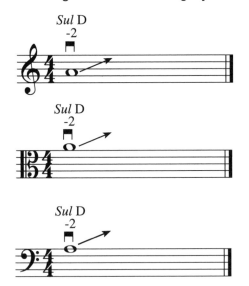

A BACKWARD VIBRATO MOTION–Gently roll the finger from the A to slightly below the A and back to the A.

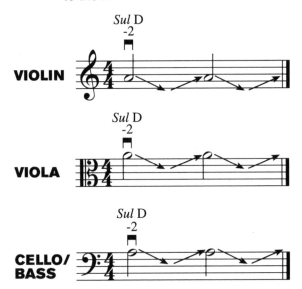

A FORWARD VIBRATO MOTION–Gently roll the finger from the A to slightly above the A and back to the A.

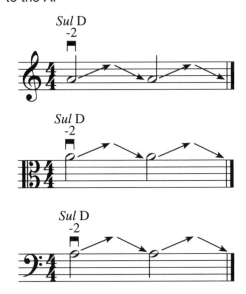

Level 3: Sound Shifting
Vibrato

52   **A COMPLETE VIBRATO MOTION**—*Starting on the note A, roll the finger backward and forward pulsing on each rhythm below.*

SOUND ADVICE

Remind students to keep the left hand relaxed.

153 **THE G MAJOR SCALE STARTING AND STOPPING VIBRATO**—*Play the the first note of every measure with* vibrato *and the second note without* vibrato.

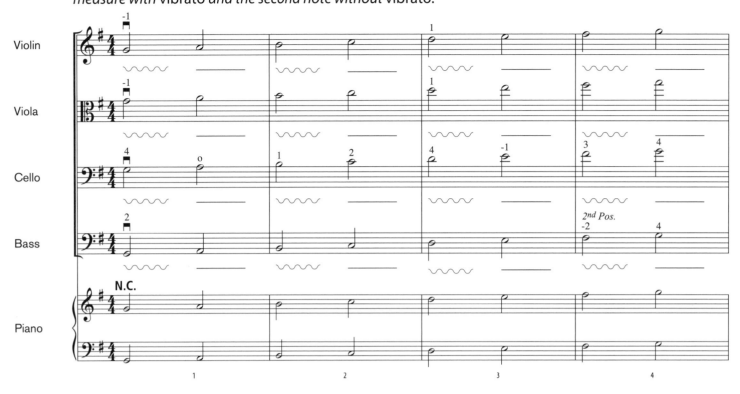

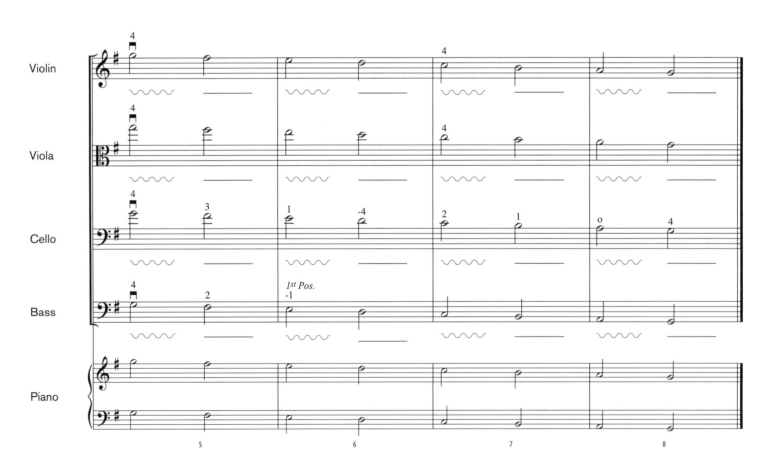

SOUND ADVICE

Remind students to keep the left hand relaxed.

54 **CHESTER WITH VIBRATO**—*Play* Chester *using* vibrato.

William Billings

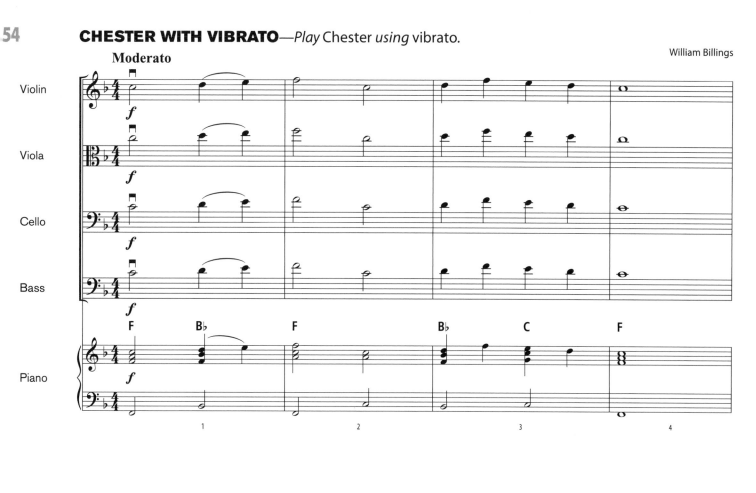

SOUND ADVICE

Remind students to keep the left hand relaxed.

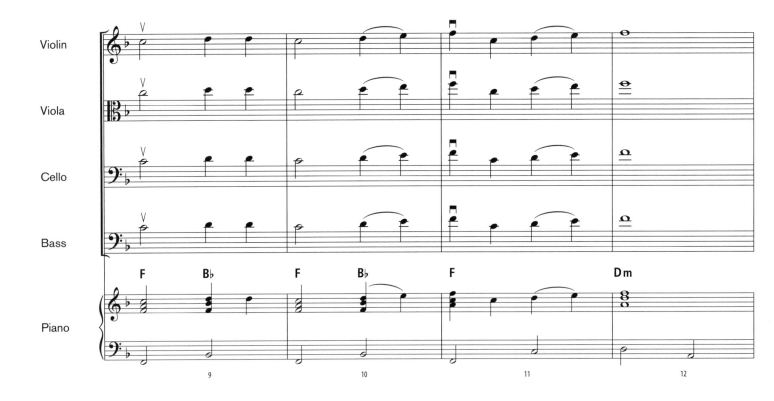

Level 4: Sound Scales, Arpeggios, Chorales & Rhythms

C Major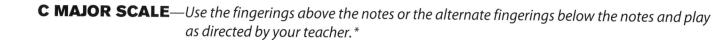
View video at
alfred.com/SoundDevelopmentVideo

155 **C MAJOR SCALE**—*Use the fingerings above the notes or the alternate fingerings below the notes and play as directed by your teacher.* *

SOUND ADVICE

Remind students to follow all fingerings.

* Basses have one set of fingerings for each scale.

156 **C MAJOR ARPEGGIO**—*Play as directed by your teacher.*

SOUND ADVICE

Remind students to follow all fingerings.

157 ## C MAJOR SCALE IN THIRDS—*Play as directed by your teacher.*

SOUND ADVICE

Remind students to follow all fingerings.

158   **C MAJOR BOWING VARIATIONS**—*Play the C major scale using the bowing variations below.*

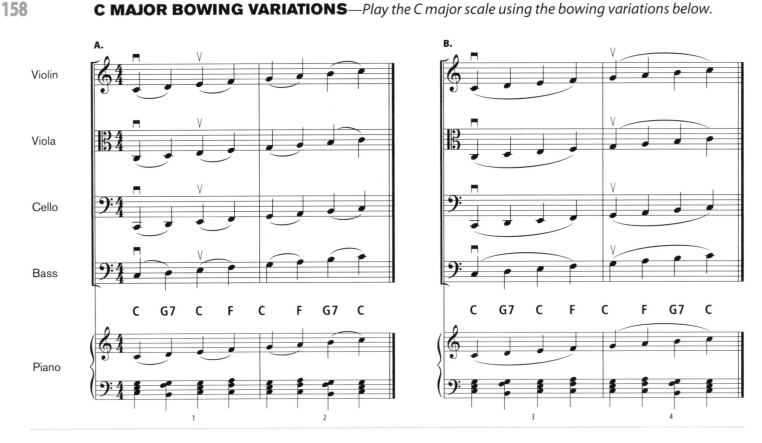

SOUND ADVICE

Remind students to follow the bowings.

159   **C MAJOR SCALE ACCOMPANIMENTS**—*Take turns accompanying the scale above using either the harmonized or drone accompaniment.*

Challenge: Listen to the ensemble as the class plays the scale and accompaniment together. Aurally identify which part is the scale and which part is the accompaniment.

SOUND ADVICE

Remind students to balance the chords.

Level 4: Sound Scales, Arpeggios, Chorales & Rhythms
A Natural Minor

160   **A NATURAL MINOR SCALE**—*Use the fingerings above the notes or the alternate fingerings below the notes and play as directed by your teacher.*

SOUND ADVICE

Remind students to follow all fingerings.

161 A NATURAL MINOR ARPEGGIO—*Play as directed by your teacher.*

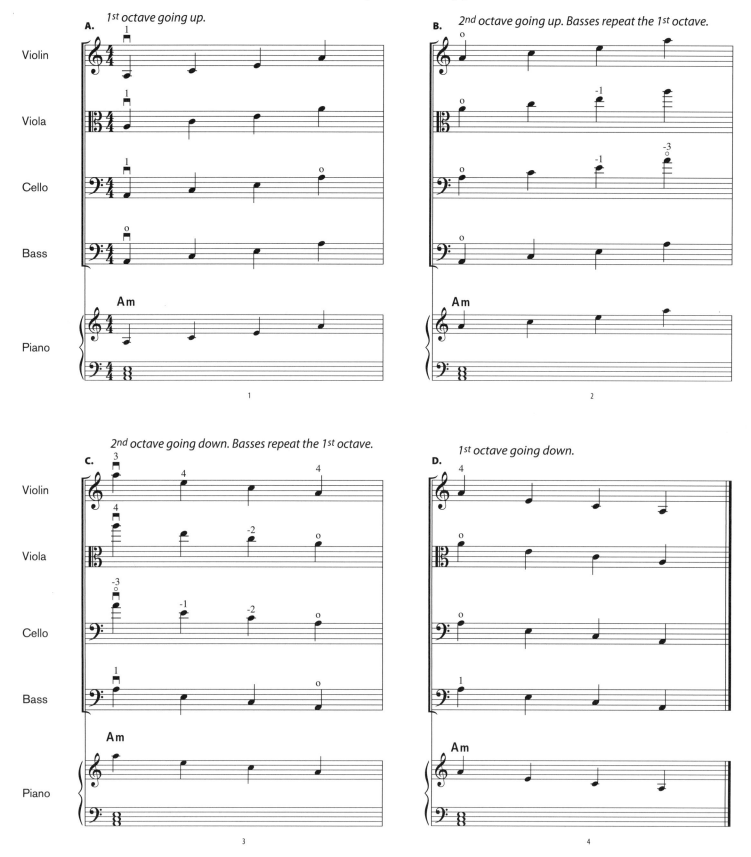

SOUND ADVICE

Remind students to follow all fingerings.

A NATURAL MINOR SCALE IN THIRDS—*Play as directed by your teacher.*

SOUND ADVICE

Remind students to follow all fingerings.

163   **A NATURAL MINOR BOWING VARIATIONS**—*Play the A natural minor scale using the bowing variations below.*

SOUND ADVICE

Remind students to follow the bowings.

164   **A NATURAL MINOR SCALE ACCOMPANIMENTS**—*Take turns accompanying the scale above using either the harmonized or drone accompaniment.*

Challenge: Identify the intervals being used in the A Natural Minor Arpeggio exercise.

SOUND ADVICE

Remind students to balance the chords.

Level 4: Sound Scales, Arpeggios, Chorales & Rhythms
G Major

165

G MAJOR SCALE—*Use the fingerings above the notes or the alternate fingerings below the notes and play as directed by your teacher.*

SOUND ADVICE

Remind students to follow all fingerings.

166 **G MAJOR ARPEGGIO**—*Play as directed by your teacher.*

SOUND ADVICE

Remind students to follow all fingerings.

67 **G MAJOR SCALE IN THIRDS**—*Play as directed by your teacher.*

SOUND ADVICE

Remind students to follow all fingerings.

168   **G MAJOR BOWING VARIATIONS**—*Play the G major scale using the bowing variations below.*

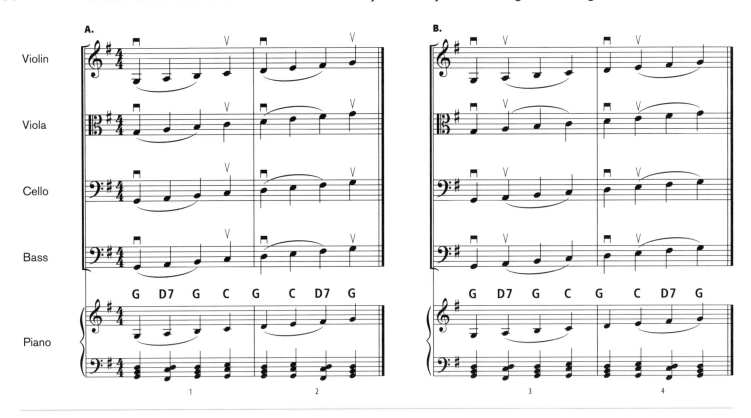

SOUND ADVICE

Remind students to follow the bowings.

169   **G MAJOR SCALE ACCOMPANIMENTS**—*Take turns accompanying the scale above using either the harmonized or drone accompaniment.*

Challenge: Identify which part of the chord you are playing on each quarter note in the harmonized accompaniment.

SOUND ADVICE

Remind students to balance the chords.

Level 4: Sound Scales, Arpeggios, Chorales & Rhythms
E Natural Minor

E NATURAL MINOR SCALE—*Use the fingerings above the notes or the alternate fingerings below the notes and play as directed by your teacher.*

SOUND ADVICE

Remind students to follow all fingerings.

171   **E NATURAL MINOR ARPEGGIO**—*Play as directed by your teacher.*

SOUND ADVICE

Remind students to follow all fingerings.

E NATURAL MINOR SCALE IN THIRDS—*Play as directed by your teacher.*

SOUND ADVICE

Remind students to follow all fingerings.

173 **E NATURAL MINOR BOWING VARIATIONS**—*Play the E natural minor scale using the bowing variations below.*

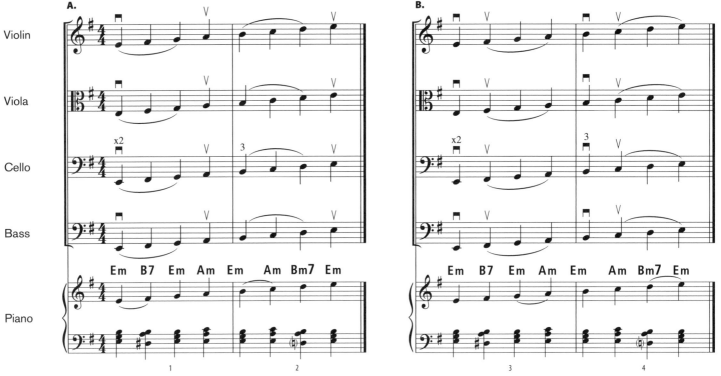

SOUND ADVICE

Remind students to follow the bowings.

174 **E NATURAL MINOR SCALE ACCOMPANIMENTS**—*Take turns accompanying the scale above using either the harmonized or drone accompaniment.*

Challenge: By ear, indentify each interval you play while using the drone accompaniment with the scale.

SOUND ADVICE

Remind students to balance the chords.

Level 4: Sound Scales, Arpeggios, Chorales & Rhythms
D Major

175 **D MAJOR SCALE**—*Use the fingerings above the notes or the alternate fingerings below the notes and play as directed by your teacher.*

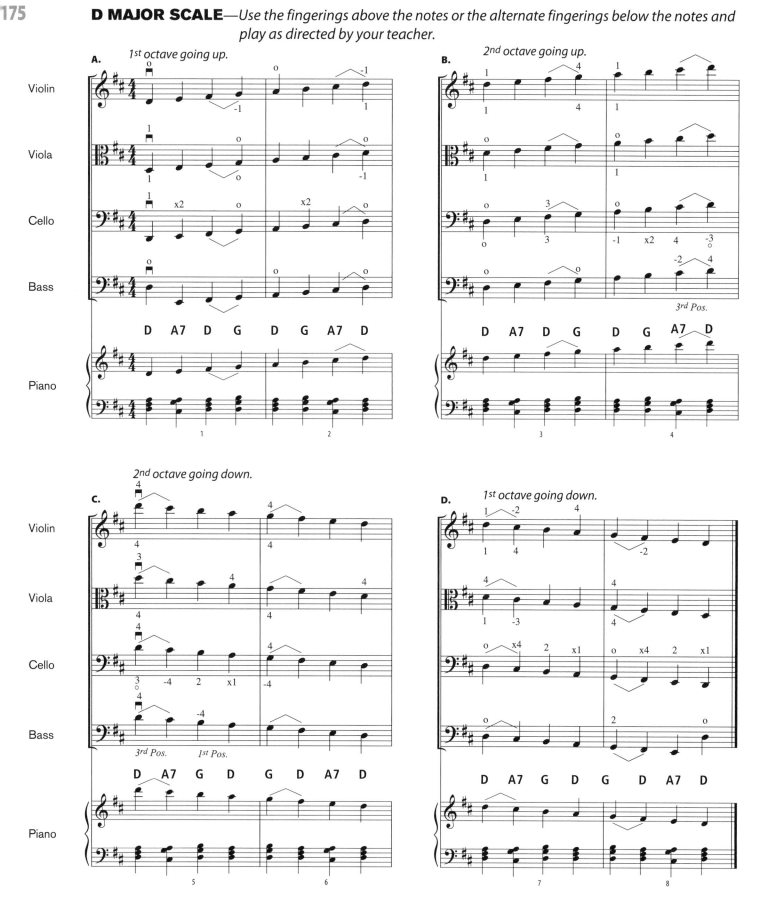

SOUND ADVICE

Remind students to follow all fingerings.

176 **D MAJOR ARPEGGIO**—*Play as directed by your teacher.*

SOUND ADVICE

Remind students to follow all fingerings.

177 **D MAJOR SCALE IN THIRDS**—*Play as directed by your teacher.*

SOUND ADVICE

Remind students to follow all fingerings.

178 **D MAJOR BOWING VARIATIONS**—*Play the D major scale using the bowing variations below.*

SOUND ADVICE

Remind students to follow the bowings.

179 **D MAJOR SCALE ACCOMPANIMENTS**—*Take turns accompanying the scale above using either the harmonized or drone accompaniment.*

Challenge: Record yourself playing the D major scale and evalute your performance for intonation.

SOUND ADVICE

Remind students to balance the chords.

Level 4: Sound Scales, Arpeggios, Chorales & Rhythms
B Natural Minor

180

B NATURAL MINOR SCALE—*Use the fingerings above the notes or the alternate fingerings below the notes and play as directed by your teacher.*

SOUND ADVICE

Remind students to follow all fingerings.

181 B NATURAL MINOR ARPEGGIO—*Play as directed by your teacher.*

SOUND ADVICE

Remind students to follow all fingerings.

B NATURAL MINOR SCALE IN THIRDS—*Play as directed by your teacher.*

SOUND ADVICE

Remind students to follow all fingerings.

183 **B NATURAL MINOR BOWING VARIATIONS**—*Play the B natural minor scale using the bowing variations below.*

SOUND ADVICE

Remind students to follow the bowings.

184 **B NATURAL MINOR SCALE ACCOMPANIMENTS**—*Take turns accompanying the scale above using either the harmonized or drone accompaniment.*

Challenge: Record yourself playing the B natural minor scale and evaluate your performance for rhythmic stability.

SOUND ADVICE

Remind students to balance the chords.

Level 4: Sound Scales, Arpeggios, Chorales & Rhythms
A Major

185

A MAJOR SCALE—*Use the fingerings above the notes or the alternate fingerings below the notes and play as directed by your teacher.*

SOUND ADVICE

Remind students to follow all fingerings.

186 **A MAJOR ARPEGGIO**—*Play as directed by your teacher.*

SOUND ADVICE

Remind students to follow all fingerings.

A MAJOR SCALE IN THIRDS—*Play as directed by your teacher.*

SOUND ADVICE

Remind students to follow all fingerings.

188   **A MAJOR BOWING VARIATIONS**—*Play the A major scale using the bowing variations below.*

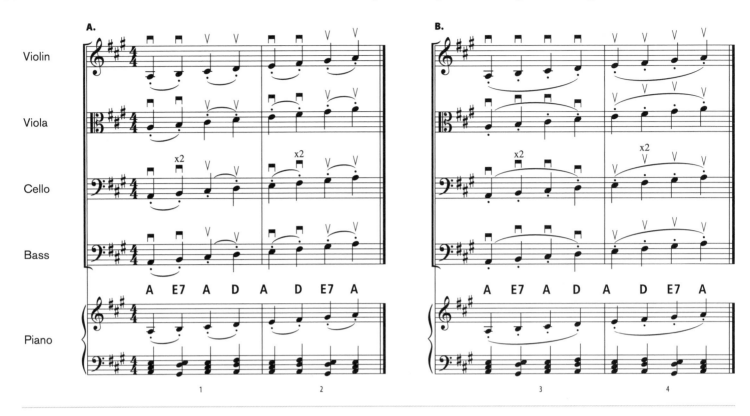

SOUND ADVICE

Remind students to follow the bowings.

189   **A MAJOR SCALE ACCOMPANIMENTS**—*Take turns accompanying the scale above using either the harmonized or drone accompaniment.*

Challenge: Perform the A major scale in a round with your stand partner and listen for good intonation.

SOUND ADVICE

Remind students to balance the chords.

Level 4: Sound Scales, Arpeggios, Chorales & Rhythms
F Major

F MAJOR SCALE—*Use the fingerings above the notes or the alternate fingerings below the notes and play as directed by your teacher.*

SOUND ADVICE

Remind students to follow all fingerings.

191   **F MAJOR ARPEGGIO**—*Play as directed by your teacher.*

SOUND ADVICE

Remind students to follow all fingerings.

F MAJOR SCALE IN THIRDS—*Play as directed by your teacher.*

SOUND ADVICE

Remind students to follow all fingerings.

193 **F MAJOR BOWING VARIATIONS**—*Play the F major scale using the bowing variations below.*

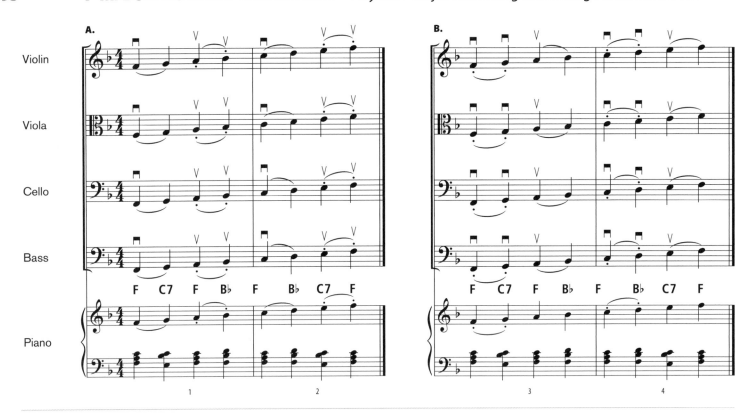

SOUND ADVICE

Remind students to follow the bowings.

194 **F MAJOR SCALE ACCOMPANIMENTS**—*Take turns accompanying the scale above using either the harmonized or drone accompaniment.*

Challenge: Play the F major scale and arpeggio from memory.

SOUND ADVICE

Remind students to balance the chords.

Level 4: Sound Scales, Arpeggios, Chorales & Rhythms
D Natural Minor

D NATURAL MINOR SCALE—*Use the fingerings above the notes or the alternate fingerings below the notes and play as directed by your teacher.*

SOUND ADVICE

Remind students to follow all fingerings.

196 **D NATURAL MINOR ARPEGGIO**—*Play as directed by your teacher.*

SOUND ADVICE

Remind students to follow all fingerings.

197 D NATURAL MINOR SCALE IN THIRDS—*Play as directed by your teacher.*

SOUND ADVICE

Remind students to follow all fingerings.

198 D NATURAL MINOR BOWING VARIATIONS—*Play the D natural minor scale using the bowing variations below.*

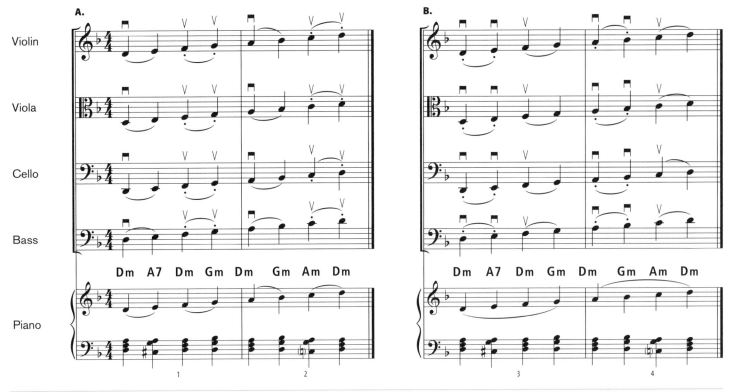

SOUND ADVICE

Remind students to follow the bowings.

199 D NATURAL MINOR SCALE ACCOMPANIMENTS—*Take turns accompanying the scale above using either the harmonized or drone accompaniment.*

Challenge: Play the D natural minor scale with a metronome. Start at a slow tempo and work to a faster tempo

SOUND ADVICE

Remind students to balance the chords.

Level 4: Sound Scales, Arpeggios, Chorales & Rhythms
Bb Major

Bb MAJOR SCALE—*Use the fingerings above the notes or the alternate fingerings below the notes and play as directed by your teacher.*

SOUND ADVICE

Remind students to follow all fingerings.

201 **B♭ MAJOR ARPEGGIO**—*Play as directed by your teacher.*

SOUND ADVICE

Remind students to follow all fingerings.

B♭ MAJOR SCALE IN THIRDS—*Play as directed by your teacher.*

SOUND ADVICE

Remind students to follow all fingerings.

203 B♭ MAJOR BOWING VARIATIONS—*Play the B♭ major scale using the bowing variations below.*

SOUND ADVICE

Remind students to follow the bowings.

204 B♭ MAJOR SCALE ACCOMPANIMENTS—*Take turns accompanying the scale above using either the harmonized or drone accompaniment.*

Challenge: Take turns playing the B♭ Major Scale In Thirds and the Drone Accompaniment with your stand partner. Listen for good intonation.

SOUND ADVICE

Remind students to balance the chords.

Level 4: Sound Scales, Arpeggios, Chorales & Rhythms
G Natural Minor

G NATURAL MINOR SCALE—*Use the fingerings above the notes or the alternate fingerings below the notes and play as directed by your teacher.*

SOUND ADVICE

Remind students to follow all fingerings.

206   **G NATURAL MINOR ARPEGGIO**—*Play as directed by your teacher.*

SOUND ADVICE

Remind students to follow all fingerings.

G NATURAL MINOR SCALE IN THIRDS—*Play as directed by your teacher.*

A. *1st octave going up.*

B. *2nd octave going up.*

C. *2nd octave going down.*

D. *1st octave going down.*

SOUND ADVICE

Remind students to follow all fingerings.

208 G NATURAL MINOR BOWING VARIATIONS—*Play the G natural minor scale using the bowing variations below.*

SOUND ADVICE

Remind students to follow the bowings.

209 G NATURAL MINOR SCALE ACCOMPANIMENTS—*Take turns accompanying the scale above using either the harmonized or drone accompaniment.*

Challenge: Play the G natural minor scale using bowing patterns from some of the other scales.

SOUND ADVICE

Remind students to balance the chords.

Level 4: Sound Scales, Arpeggios, Chorales & Rhythms
E♭ Major

E♭ MAJOR SCALE—*Use the fingerings above the notes or alternate fingerings below the notes and play as directed by your teacher.*

SOUND ADVICE

Remind students to follow all fingerings.

210 E♭ MAJOR ARPEGGIO—*Play as directed by your teacher.*

SOUND ADVICE

Remind students to follow all fingerings.

.12

E♭ MAJOR SCALE IN THIRDS—*Play as directed by your teacher.*

SOUND ADVICE

Remind students to follow all fingerings.

E♭ MAJOR BOWING VARIATIONS—*Play the E♭ major scale using the bowing variations below.*

SOUND ADVICE

Remind students to follow the bowings.

214

E♭ MAJOR SCALE ACCOMPANIMENTS—*Take turns accompanying the scale above using either the harmonized or drone accompaniment.*

Challenge: Take turns playing the E♭ major scale holding each note as a whole note while your stand partner plays the drone accompaniment. Listen carefully for good intonation.

SOUND ADVICE

Remind students to balance the chords.

Level 4: Sound Scales, Arpeggios, Chorales & Rhythms
Major Scales

215   **C MAJOR SCALE**—*Play as directed by your teacher.*

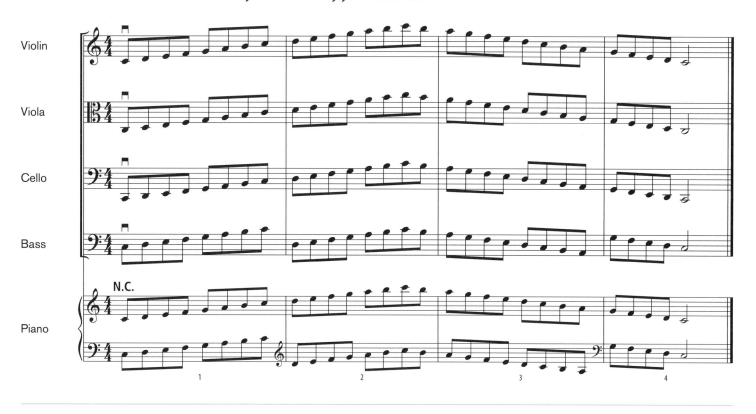

SOUND ADVICE

Ask students to choose one of the fingerings they have learned for this scale.

216   **G MAJOR SCALE**—*Play as directed by your teacher.*

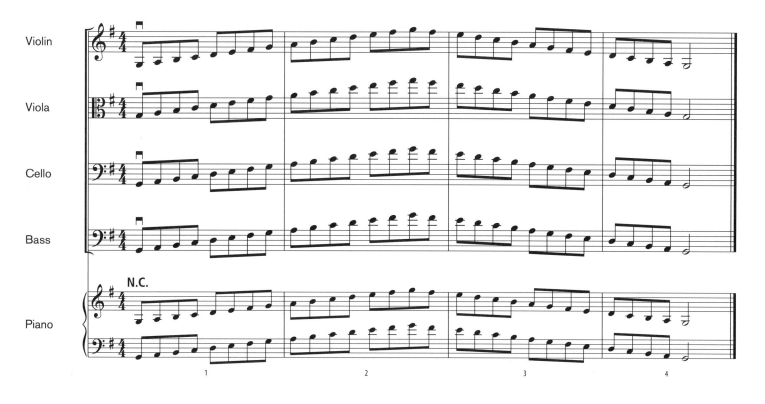

SOUND ADVICE

Ask students to choose one of the fingerings they have learned for this scale.

217 **D MAJOR SCALE**—*Play as directed by your teacher.*

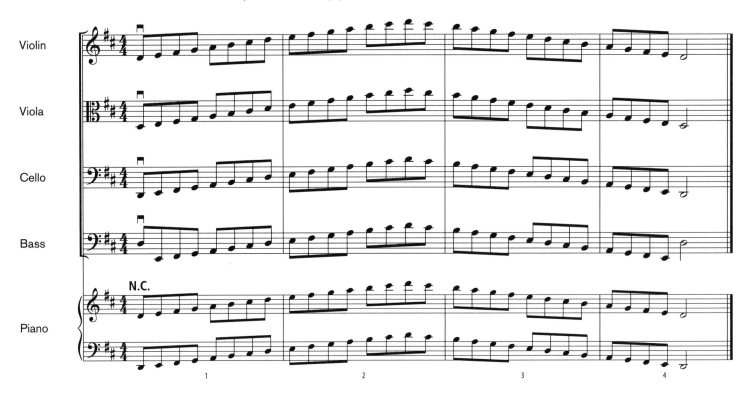

SOUND ADVICE

Ask students to choose one of the fingerings they have learned for this scale.

218 **A MAJOR SCALE**—*Play as directed by your teacher.*

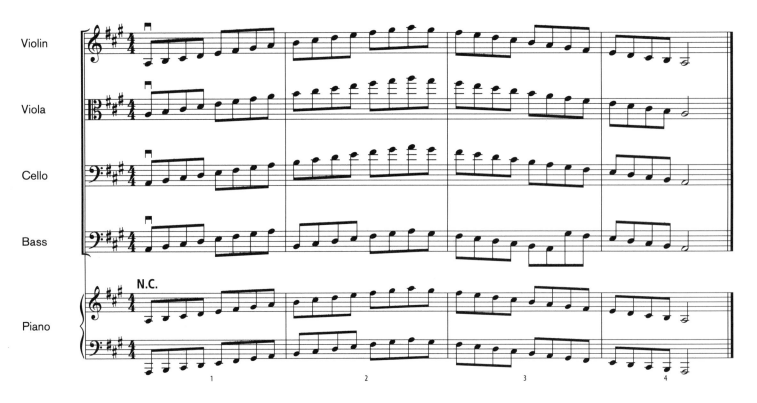

SOUND ADVICE

Ask students to choose one of the fingerings they have learned for this scale.

219   **F MAJOR SCALE**—*Play as directed by your teacher.*

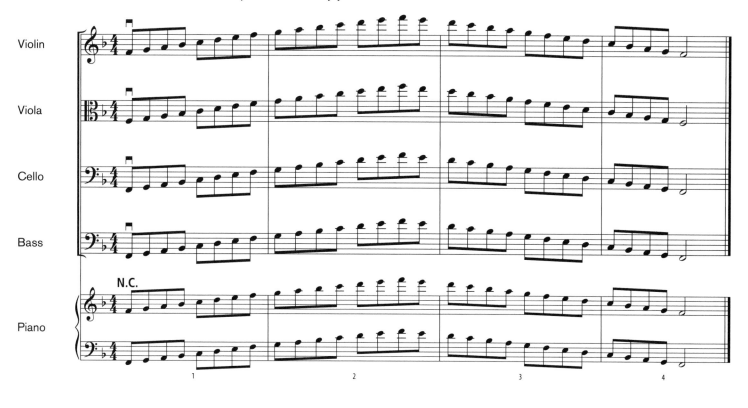

SOUND ADVICE

Ask students to choose one of the fingerings they have learned for this scale.

220   **B♭ MAJOR SCALE**—*Play as directed by your teacher.*

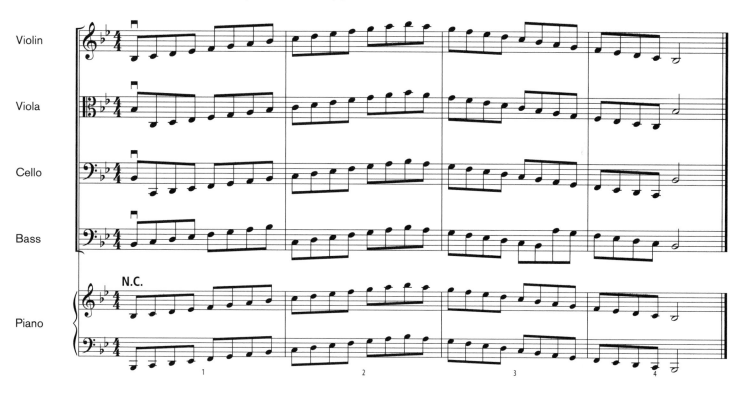

SOUND ADVICE

Ask students to choose one of the fingerings they have learned for this scale.

221 **E♭ MAJOR SCALE**—*Play as directed by your teacher.*

SOUND ADVICE

Ask students to choose one of the fingerings they have learned for this scale.

Level 4: Sound Scales, Arpeggios, Chorales & Rhythms
Minor Scales

222 **A NATURAL MINOR SCALE**—*Play as directed by your teacher.*

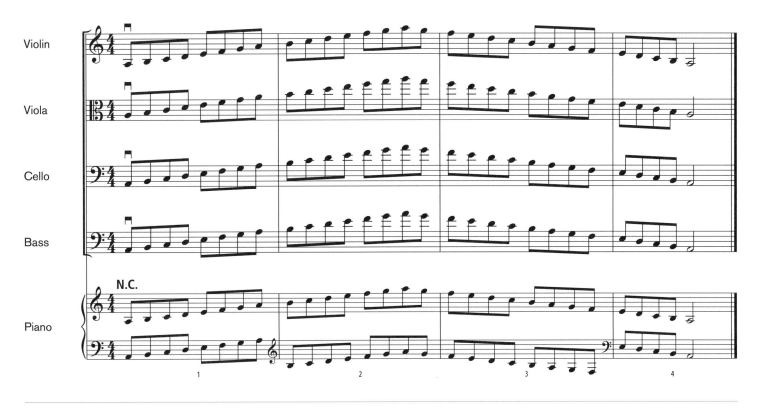

SOUND ADVICE

Ask students to choose one of the fingerings they have learned for this scale.

223 **E NATURAL MINOR SCALE**—*Play as directed by your teacher.*

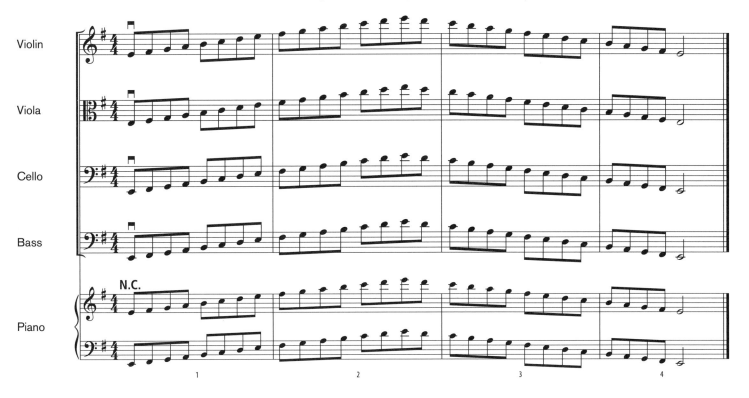

SOUND ADVICE

Ask students to choose one of the fingerings they have learned for this scale.

218

224 **B NATURAL MINOR SCALE**—*Play as directed by your teacher.*

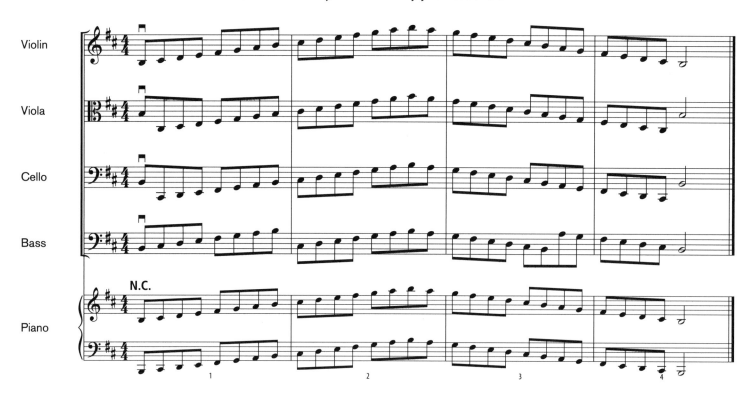

SOUND ADVICE

Ask students to choose one of the fingerings they have learned for this scale.

225 **D NATURAL MINOR SCALE**—*Play as directed by your teacher.*

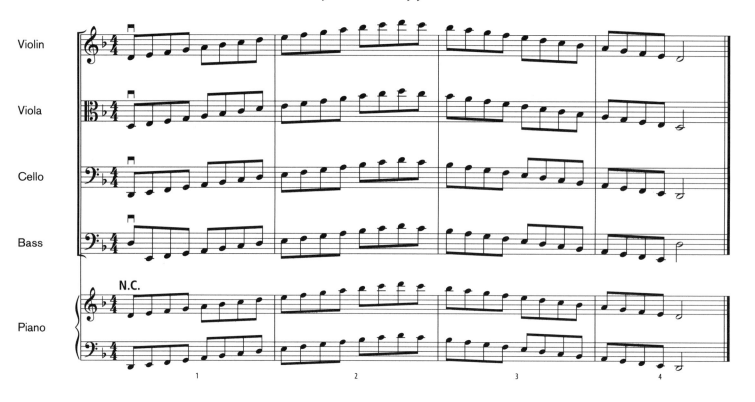

SOUND ADVICE

Ask students to choose one of the fingerings they have learned for this scale.

226   **G NATURAL MINOR SCALE**—*Play as directed by your teacher.*

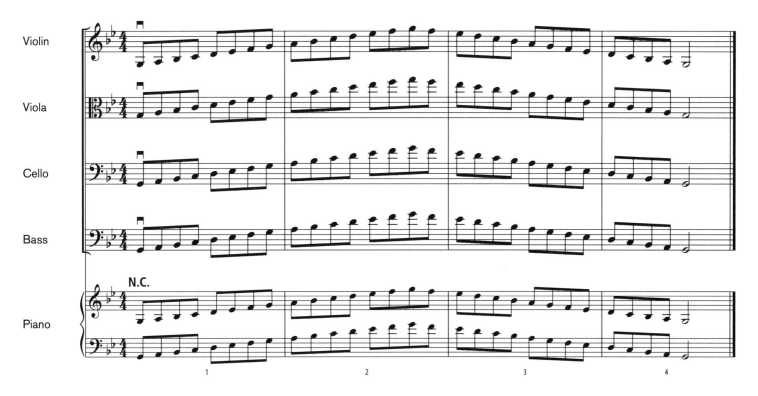

SOUND ADVICE

Ask students to choose one of the fingerings they have learned for this scale.

SIGHT-READING CHECKLIST

1. **TITLE**–check the title for information about the style or form of the piece.
2. **COMPOSER'S NAME**–check the composer's name for information about the style.
3. **TEMPOS AND TEMPO CHANGES**–check for information about the speed of the piece.
4. **KEY SIGNATURE AND KEY SIGNATURE CHANGES**–look for changes in the naturals, sharps, and flats.
5. **TIME SIGNATURE AND TIME SIGNATURE CHANGES**–check to see the number of beats in each measure and any changes.
6. **TRAFFIC PATTERNS**–check for information that indicates where to go in the music such as D.C., D.S. and repeats.
7. **DYNAMICS**–scan the piece for dynamics. Notice the beginning and ending dynamic.
8. **ACCIDENTALS**–scan the piece for accidentals.
9. **ARTICULATIONS**–scan the piece for articulations.
10. **BOWINGS**–scan the piece for special bowings and bowing patterns.
11. **POSITIONS AND FINGERINGS**–scan the piece for higher positions and finger pattern changes.

206 **SIGHT-READ IT**—*Scan the piece for each sight-reading checkpoint and then play. Evaluate your performance and decide how to improve it.*

Challenge: Use the sight-reading checklist to prepare to sight-read a piece your teacher chooses.

SOUND ADVICE

Remind students to scan ahead when sight-reading.

Level 4: Sound Scales, Arpeggios, Chorales & Rhythms
Finger Action

228 **CHROMATIC MOVEMENT**—*Violins and violas practice sliding a finger from one half step to another with precision. Cellos and basses review chromatic alterations.*

SOUND ADVICE

Remind students to keep the left-hand fingers curved.

229 **CHROMATIC SCALE**—*Practice playing a chromatic scale. Challenge: Play the alternate fingerings.*

SOUND ADVICE

Remind students to keep the left-hand fingers curved.

230   **HORIZONTAL MOVEMENT**—*Practice moving your finger horizontally from one string to the other. Lift the finger up. Basses review.*

SOUND ADVICE

Remind students to keep the left-hand fingers curved.

231   **VELOCITY EXERCISE**—*Practice lifting your left-hand fingers like a spring.*

SOUND ADVICE

Remind students to keep the left-hand fingers curved.

232 **TRILL MOTION**—*Practice the trill motion by alternating between two notes with faster and faster rhythms.*

SOUND ADVICE

Remind students to keep the left-hand fingers curved.

233 **TRILL EXERCISE**—*Practice going between the written out trill motion and the trill notation.*

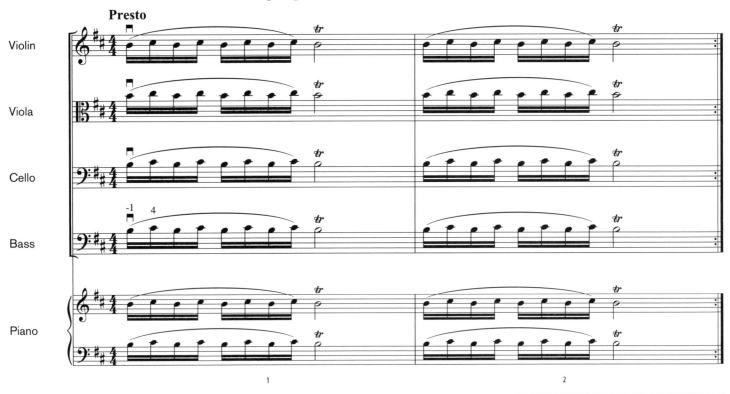

SOUND ADVICE

Remind students to keep the left-hand fingers curved.

234 **INDEPENDENT FINGER MOVEMENT**—*Violins and violas practice moving fingers independently from each other while cellos and basses reveiw.*

SOUND ADVICE

Remind students to keep the left-hand fingers curved.

Level 4: Sound Scales, Arpeggios, Chorales & Rhythms
Chorales

CHORALE NO. 1, CHRISTUS, DER IST MEIN LEBEN—*Listen to all parts and adjust your intonation to the other players. Your teacher will tell you whether to play Part A, the melody, or Part B, the accompaniment.*

Johann Sebastian Bach

SOUND ADVICE

Have students take turns performing the chorale in small groups while the rest of the class evaluates the performance.

LEARN TO READ COMBINED PART NOTATION

Sometimes two separate parts are combined on one staff. Outside players perform the notes with stems up and inside players play the notes with the stems down.

236   **CHORALE NO. 2, RHOSYMEDRE**—*Listen to all parts and adjust your intonation to the other players. Your teacher will tell you whether to play the upper part, the melody, or the lower part, the accompaniment. Write in the fingerings for the upper notes above the staff and the lower notes below the staff.*

Jonathan David Edwards

SOUND ADVICE

Have students take turns performing the chorale while the rest of the class practices good audience behavior.

Level 4: Sound Scales, Arpeggios, Chorales & Rhythms
Rhythms
Play each exercise on a note of your teacher's choice.

237 $\frac{4}{4}$ **RHYTHMS**—*Count, clap and play using a counting system of your teacher's choice. Play as a two-part round starting in a measure your teacher directs. Challenge: Compose, notate and perform your own rhythm patterns in this meter.*

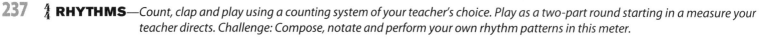

238 $\frac{3}{4}$ **RHYTHMS**—*Count, clap and play using a counting system of your teacher's choice. Challenge: Compose a rhythmic accompaniment to this exercise. Create an arrangement by assigning instruments to play either the exercise or accompaniment, then play in a three-part round and assign instruments to each part.*

239 $\frac{5}{4}$ **RHYTHMS**—*Count, clap and play using a counting system of your teacher's choice. Play as a two-part round starting in a measure your teacher directs. Challenge: Improvise your own rhythm patterns in this meter.*

240 $\frac{2}{4}$ **RHYTHMS**—*Count, clap and play using a counting system of your teacher's choice. Play as a four-part round starting in a measure your teacher directs. Challenge: Improvise your own rhythm patterns in this meter.*

241 **CUT TIME RHYTHMS**—*Count, clap and play using a counting system of your teacher's choice. Play as a four-part round starting in a measure your teacher directs. Challenge: Improvise your own rhythm patterns in this meter.*

242 $\frac{6}{8}$ **RHYTHMS**—*Count, clap and play using a counting system of your teacher's choice. Challenge: Play by ear an eight bar phrase of $\frac{6}{8}$ rhythms from any $\frac{6}{8}$ piece you know. Play by ear an eight bar phrase from different genres of music in $\frac{6}{8}$ time.*

243 $\frac{9}{8}$ **RHYTHMS**—*Count, clap and play using a counting system of your teacher's choice. Take turns playing the $\frac{9}{8}$ rhythms for your stand partner and then evalute the quality and effectiveness of your peformances.*

244 $\frac{5}{8}$ **RHYTHMS**—*Count, clap and play using a counting system of your teacher's choice. Challenge: Write and perform your own rhythm patterns in this meter.*

245 $\frac{7}{8}$ **RHYTHMS**—*Count, clap and play using a counting system of your teacher's choice. Challenge: Write and perform your own rhythm patterns in this meter.*